2

INSIDE WRITING

The Academic Word List in Context

Jennifer Bixby

Nigel A. Caplan

SERIES DIRECTOR:

Cheryl Boyd Zimmerman

OXFORD

UNIVERSITY PRESS

OXFORD
UNIVERSITY PRESS

198 Madison Avenue
New York, NY 10016 USA

Great Clarendon Street, Oxford, OX2 6DP, United Kingdom

Oxford University Press is a department of the University of Oxford.
It furthers the University's objective of excellence in research, scholarship,
and education by publishing worldwide. Oxford is a registered trade
mark of Oxford University Press in the UK and in certain other countries

Director, ELT New York: Laura Pearson
Head of Adult, ELT New York: Stephanie Karras
Senior Development Editor: Wiley Gaby
Executive Art and Design Manager: Maj-Britt Hagsted
Design Project Manager: Michael Steinhofer
Content Production Manager: Julie Armstrong
Production Artist: Julie Sussman-Perez
Image Manager: Trisha Masterson
Production Coordinator: Christopher Espejo

ISBN: 978 0 19 460126 9 STUDENT BOOK

Printed in China

This book is printed on paper from certified and well-managed sources

ACKNOWLEDGEMENTS

*The authors and publisher are grateful to those who have given permission to reproduce
the following extracts and adaptations of copyright material:*

*p. 17 Adaptation of "About Us", http://www.nomnomtruck.com. Reprinted by
permission of Citrus Studios.*

Illustration by: 5W Infographics, pgs. 12, 86, 96, 129.

*We would also like to thank the following for permission to reproduce the following
photographs*: **Cover**, Datacraft - Sozaijiten / Alamy; Shaun Egan/JAI/Corbis;
Glowimages / Corbis; Antar Dayal / Getty Images; Wolfgang Kaehler / Corbis;
Soyka / shutterstock; Valerie Potapova / shutterstock; Jennifer Gottschalk /
shutterstock. **Interior**, p1 Jennifer Gottschalk/Shutterstock (Background);
p1 John Woodworth/Alamy (Millau Viaduct); p2 Paul Carstairs/Alamy; p3 Rob
MacDougall/Getty Images; p10 Photodisc/Oxford University Press; p15 Imagno/
Getty Images; p16 Radu Razvan/Shutterstock; p17 Noah K. Murray/Star Ledger/
Corbis UK Ltd (model); p17 Dinner, Allison/the food passi/Corbis UK Ltd (food);
p25 Goodluz/Shutterstock; p29 Michael Steinhofer/Oxford University Press;
p30 Ambient Weather; p31 LesPalenik/Shutterstock (Emergency radio); p31
Midland Radio Corporation (Red alert); p35 Oprea Florin/Alamy; p41 Creative
Crop/Getty Images; p43 TrotzOlga/Shutterstock; p44 John Warburton-Lee
Photography/Alamy; p54 Brian Jackson/Alamy; p57 ra2studio/Shutterstock;
p58 M. Scott Brauer/Alamy; p59 pio3/Shutterstock; p66 nobleIMAGES/Alamy;
p71 kazoka/Shutterstock; p72 Gary Conner/Getty Images; p85 Ailani Graphics/
Shutterstock; p86 Tsuneo Yamashita/Getty Images; p94 RGB Ventures LLC
dba SuperStock/Alamy; p99 Cultura Creative (RF)/Alamy; p100 Wavebreak
Media ltd/Alamy (smartphones); p100 Blend Images/Alamy (science); p110
MBI/Oxford University Press; p113 myphotostop /iStockphoto; p114 Kaehler,
Wolfgang/Superstock Ltd.; p127 piotr_pabijan/Shutterstock; p128 Kheng Guan
Toh/Shutterstock.

Acknowledgements

We would like to acknowledge the following individuals for their input during the development of the series:

Salam Affouneh
Higher Colleges of Technology
Abu Dhabi, U.A.E.

Kristin Bouton
Intensive English Institute
Illinois, U.S.A.

Nicole H. Carrasquel
Center for Multilingual Multicultural Studies
Florida, U.S.A.

Elaine Cockerham
Higher College of Technology
Muscat, Oman

Danielle Dilkes
CultureWorks English as a Second Language Inc.
Ontario, Canada

Susan Donaldson
Tacoma Community College
Washington, U.S.A

Penelope Doyle
Higher Colleges of Technology
Dubai, U.A.E.

Edward Roland Gray
Yonsei University
Seoul, South Korea

Melanie Golbert
Higher Colleges of Technology
Abu Dhabi, U.A.E.

Elise Harbin
Alabama Language Institute
Alabama, U.S.A.

Bill Hodges
University of Guelph
Ontario, Canada

David Daniel Howard
National Chiayi University
Chiayi

Leander Hughes
Saitama Daigaku
Saitama, Japan

James Ishler
Higher Colleges of Technology
Fujairah, U.A.E.

John Iveson
Sheridan College
Ontario, Canada

Alan Lanes
Higher Colleges of Technology
Dubai, U.A.E.

Corinne Marshall
Fanshawe College
Ontario, Canada

Christine Matta
College of DuPage
Illinois, U.S.A.

Beth Montag
University at Kearney
Nebraska, U.S.A.

Kevin Mueller
Tokyo International University
Saitama, Japan

Tracy Anne Munteanu
Higher Colleges of Technology
Fujairah, U.A.E.

Eileen O'Brien
Khalifa University of Science, Technology, and Research
Sharjah, U.A.E.

Jangyo Parsons
Kookmin University
Seoul, South Korea

John P. Racine
Dokkyo Daigaku
Soka City, Japan

Scott Rousseau
American University of Sharjah
Sharjah, U.A.E.

Jane Ryther
American River College
California, U.S.A

Kate Tindle
Zayed University
Dubai, U.A.E.

Melody Traylor
Higher Colleges of Technology
Fujairah, U.A.E.

John Vogels
Higher Colleges of Technology
Dubai, U.A.E.

Kelly Wharton
Fanshawe College
Ontario, Canada

Contents

The Inside Track to Academic Success

Student Books

For additional student resources visit: www.oup.com/elt/insidewriting

iTools for all levels

The *Inside Writing* iTools is for use with an LCD projector or interactive whiteboard.

Resources for whole-class presentation

> **Book-on-screen** focuses class on teaching points and facilitates classroom management.
> **Writing worksheets** provide additional practice with the genre and Writing Models.

Resources for assessment and preparation

> Customizable Unit, Mid-term, and Final Tests evaluate student progress.
> Answer Keys and Teaching Notes

Additional instructor resources at: www.oup.com/elt/teacher/insidewriting

UNIT 1

A Bridge to the Future

In this unit, you will

> analyze a narrative and learn how they are used in architectural descriptions.
> use narrative and descriptive writing.
> increase your understanding of the target academic words for this unit.

WRITING SKILLS

> Analyzing a Narrative
> Paragraph Structure
> **GRAMMAR** Simple Past and Present Perfect

Self-Assessment

Think about how well you know each target word, and check (✓) the appropriate column. I have…

TARGET WORDS	never seen this word before.	heard or seen the word but am not sure what it means.	heard or seen the word and understand what it means.	used the word confidently in *either* speaking or writing.
AWL				
🔑 approximate				
🔑 construct				
controversy				
detect				
evident				
format				
globe				
interact				
🔑 occur				
🔑 phase				
so-called				
tense				

🔑 Oxford 3000™ keywords

Building Knowledge

Read these questions. Discuss your answers in a small group.

1. What kinds of stories do you like to read?

2. What are some differences between fiction stories and nonfiction stories?

3. What makes a nonfiction story interesting to you?

Writing Model

A narrative is a story, or a description of events. Read this narrative about a surprising bridge in London, England.

The Wobbly Bridge: A London Landmark

If you walk along the River Thames in London, you'll find beautiful gardens, many top tourist attractions, and the beautiful Millennium Bridge. This low, sleek bridge is 330 meters long. The **so-called** "blade[1] of light," a reference to
5 the **format** of the bridge, links London's financial district to the popular South Bank with its theaters, museums, and galleries. Although there are many bridges across the Thames, the Millennium Bridge is special. It was the first new pedestrian bridge built in London for over a century, and it is an amazing
10 work of engineering. But it has become most famous to Londoners because of its nickname: the Wobbly[2] Bridge.

The story of the Millennium Bridge began in 1996. A British newspaper, the local government in London, and the Royal Institute of British Architects created a competition to
15 **construct** a new bridge to cross the Thames. The plan was to open the bridge in time for January 1, 2000, the first day of the new millennium.[3] The winners of the competition had an original design. Their bridge was low without cables above the surface, so pedestrians could see the London skyline.

---
[1] *blade:* the sharp part of a knife
[2] *wobbly:* moving in an unsteady way from side to side
[3] *the millennium:* the period of time when one period of 1,000 years ends and another begins; often refers to the year 2000

20 **Construction** began in 1999, but building stopped soon after it started. The builders discovered the remains of buildings from the Middle Ages[4] during the preparation **phase** of the project! Work began again and continued all year. Unfortunately, the engineers did not quite meet the January 1 deadline. However, the new bridge opened to the public during London's Millennium celebrations on June 10, 2000.

25 Then the problems and the **controversy** started. Londoners were very excited about their new bridge, and **approximately** 80,000 people crossed the bridge on its first day. This led to an unusual effect. All bridges move a little when people walk on them, but the Millennium Bridge swayed[5] left and right a lot. Some people felt sick. Others grabbed the side of the bridge for safety. The bridge moved like a boat in rough water. After two days of unpredictable swinging and swaying, the embarrassed

30 engineers closed the bridge. The British newspapers excitedly declared the project a failure.

Researchers at Imperial College, London, studied the bridge for the next three months. They found that the problem was the people, not the bridge. In a crowd, people often walk at the same speed as others around them. Most of us sway a little from side to side as we walk. This swaying caused the bridge to move very slightly. When the bridge started moving, the people naturally followed the

35 rhythm of the bridge. They swayed even more. Of course, they all continued to walk and sway in about the same rhythm. The **interaction** of the people and the bridge made the movement more noticeable. As a result, many thought that the bridge was "wobbly." Although this effect can **occur** with any bridge, the **tension** in the cables supporting the Millennium Bridge made the swaying more

40 **evident**. Engineers spent most of 2001 adding special devices to the bridge to correct the problem. They asked groups of volunteers to walk across the bridge together and see if they could **detect** any motion. Eventually, the bridge reopened in February 2002

45 without a wobble.

After a difficult beginning, the Millennium Bridge has become a popular tourist attraction. People from all over the **globe** visit the bridge. Walking across the Millennium Bridge today, you won't feel

50 any movement, but you will enjoy wonderful views of London.

---

[4] *Middle Ages:* the period in European history from about CE 1100 to CE 1500
[5] *sway:* move or swing slowly from side to side

LEARN

A narrative, or story, is a description of events. Narratives often describe important events or a problem in the past. Most narratives also tell you the solution to the problem or the ending to the story. To tell a narrative effectively:

- introduce the subject of the narrative.

- describe the setting (time and place).

- give background information about the people or subject that you're writing about.

- describe events in time order.

- explain an important problem and its solution.

- provide a clear ending or conclusion.

APPLY

A. Write the number of the paragraph(s) where you can find the following information in the narrative.

___4___ a. explanation of the main problem

_____ b. description of the subject

_____ c. introduction of the subject

_____ d. description of the setting

_____ e. the solution to the problem

_____ f. conclusion

B. Complete the timeline with information about the Millennium Bridge.

July 1996: Competition for a new bridge

1999: _____

January 1, 2000: The "Millennium"

June 10, 2000: _____

June 12, 2000: _____

July–September 2000: _____

May 2001–January 2002: Changes made to the bridge

_____: Bridge reopens

Analyze

A. Match the underlined verbs to the correct verb tense.

_____ 1. The controversy <u>started</u>.

_____ 2. It <u>has become</u> famous.

_____ 3. It <u>is</u> a low, sleek bridge.

a. simple present

b. simple past

c. present perfect

B. Complete the chart with two more examples of each verb tense from the writing model. Share your examples and discuss the questions below in a small group.

Tense	Example
Simple present	
Simple past	
Present perfect	

1. Where in the narrative does the writer use simple present and present perfect verbs?

2. Where in the narrative does the writer use simple past verbs?

3. Why does the writer change tense in the last paragraph?

C. Discuss these questions with a partner.

1. Why do you think the writer uses *you* in the first and last paragraphs, but not in the body paragraphs?

_____

_____

2. What words does the writer use to introduce the main problem in the narrative?

_____

3. What are some words and phrases in the model that show time and the order of events?

_____

_____

Word Form Chart			
Noun	**Verb**	**Adjective**	**Adverb**
approximation	approximate	approximate	approximately
controversy	_____	controversial uncontroversial	controversially
detection detective	detect	detectable	_____
globe	_____	global	globally
occurrence	occur	_____	_____

A. Complete each sentence with the correct word form from the chart. Use the words in parentheses as clues.

1. Some new buildings cause a(an) <u>controversy</u> because they are so unusual.
   (argument)

2. Problems can _____ when bad weather hits long bridges.
   (happen)

3. Special sensors in some bridges can _____ storms and earthquakes.
   (notice)

4. There are _____ 20 bridges across the Thames.
   (about)

5. _____, there are many amazing bridges.
   (around the world)

6. The decision to build the bridge was _____.
   (not popular with everyone)

In chemistry, two things can *interact* during an experiment. People can also *interact* with each other.

> Rust is the result of water **interacting** with a metal such as iron.

> I **interact** with people from four different countries at my job.

An *interaction* occurs when two things are mixed together or two people work or talk together.

> The **interaction** between the bridge and its visitors created a problem.

Something that is *interactive* involves people working or talking together.

> In an **interactive** class, the teacher and the students all have a chance to talk.

 CORPUS

B. Choose the correct word to complete each sentence.

1. The museum presents an (*interact* /(*interactive*)) display about the construction of the bridge.

2. The weather (*interacted* / *interacting*) with the type of steel in the bridge.

3. The (*interactive / interaction*) between the people's footsteps and the bridge's rhythm caused the movement.

4. The sun and the sea (*interact / interaction*) to damage bridges.

5. People do not usually (*interaction / interact*) with each other when they cross bridges.

6. My class isn't (*interactive / interaction*) because the teacher lectures all the time.

C. Match the verb to the appropriate phrase.

_b_ 1. interact	a. in 2006
_____ 2. occurred	b. with other people
_____ 3. detect	c. his whole body
_____ 4. format	d. problems
_____ 5. tensed	e. a new bridge
_____ 6. construct	f. your homework

Vocabulary Activities **STEP II: Sentence Level**

D. Write a sentence with each verb and phrase from activity C.

1. *A good manager can interact well with other people.* _____

2. _____

3. _____

4. _____

5. _____

6. _____

The adjective *so-called* has two different meanings. It can introduce the word that people usually use to describe something.

> *The gap between the Baby Boomers and the **so-called** Generation Y is getting wider.*

So-called can show that you don't think a description of something or someone is appropriate.

> *Ordinary farmers know much more about this than the **so-called** "experts."*

CORPUS

E. Rewrite each sentence using *so-called*. Mark any sentences that are examples of the second definition.

1. The article is about the "Wobbly" Bridge.

> *The article is about the so-called "Wobbly" Bridge.*

2. The bridge was due to open in the year 2000, the Millennium.

_____

3. An artist made a musical exhibit using the bridge.

_____

4. The problem was caused by "lateral vibrations."

_____

5. One end of the Millennium Bridge leads to the "South Bank" area with many theaters and art museums.

_____

6. The engineers understood the project better than the team of experts.

_____

F. **Read the paragraph below. Write a sentence to answer each question. Use the target word in parentheses in your answer.**

It can be hard to find places for children to play in large cities, so the Smith Playground and Playhouse in Philadelphia is an amazing resource for families. The Smith family built the house in 1899. It is a beautiful house full of toys, bikes, and pretend cars. In addition to the house, children enjoy a huge playground. In 2004, it was clear that the playground needed improving. A group of residents collected money to update the playground. They built a new area for small children under the age of five. They also added an attractive wooden slide for older kids. In the next stage, they will add a space with water games. The playground has become very popular. Many events and even summer camps take place there regularly.

1. When did the building of the playhouse begin? (*construction*)

   Construction began in 1899.

2. What happened in 2004? (*evident*)

   _____

3. What did the group of residents build first? (*constructed*)

   _____

4. What will they add in the next stage of the project? (*phase*)

   _____

5. What happens during the summer at Smith Playground? (*occur*)

   _____

Use the simple past to tell about something that happened at a specific time in the past.

We visited the bridge in 2000.

Use the present perfect to tell about something that happened in the past, but doesn't mention a specific time.

We have visited the bridge many times.

The simple past can also be used to tell about things that started and ended in the past.

I visited England during the 2012 Olympic Games.

The present perfect can be used to tell about things that began in the past, but continue into the present.

The bridge has become a major tourist attraction.

The present perfect is often used in sentences that include prepositions of time, such as *since* and *for*.

There <u>have been</u> no problems with the bridge <u>since 2002</u>.

The bridge <u>has been</u> open <u>for</u> more than <u>ten years</u>.

Use the simple past in an adverb clause with *since*. Use the present perfect in the main clause.

main clause   adverb clause

Tourists <u>have enjoyed</u> the bridge <u>since it opened</u>.

In a narrative, writers often use the present perfect at the start of the story (What has happened before this story?) and at the end (What has happened after this story?).

A. Read this narrative about the Sydney Opera House. Look at the underlined verbs. If they are incorrect, rewrite them.

Since it opened, the Sydney Opera House ~~came~~ *has come* to represent an entire

country. This amazing building <u>has only sat</u> in Sydney's harbor for 40 years,

but in that time it <u>became</u> a symbol of Australia. In 1956 the New South

Wales government <u>has started</u> a competition to design a new opera house.

A Danish architect, Jørn Utzon, won the competition. Construction on the

Opera House <u>had began</u> in 1959 and <u>ended</u> in September 1973. Since the

Sydney Opera House <u>has opened</u>, it has received many prizes and awards.

Now, two million people see a performance there every year.

B. Complete the sentences with the simple past or present perfect form of the verb in parentheses.

1. The Sydney Harbor Bridge ___*has joined*___ the two sides of the harbor for more than 80 years.
   (join)

2. The building of the bridge _____ in 1924.
   (begin)

3. It _____ 1,400 men eight years to build the bridge.
   (take)

4. The number of vehicles on the bridge each day _____ from 11,000 in 1932 to 160,000 today.
   (increase)

5. In 1992, the city _____ a tunnel to handle the increase in traffic.
   (construct)

WRITING SKILL Paragraph Structure

LEARN

A paragraph is a connected group of sentences on the same topic or with the same purpose. In newspapers and informal writing, such as email, one-sentence paragraphs may be common. In academic writing and most other formal situations, however, paragraphs usually have more than one sentence.

In many paragraphs, the first sentence is very important. It could:

1. tell the reader the topic of the paragraph. (*The Millennium Bridge is one of London's most famous sights.*)

2. link the paragraph to the previous paragraph. (*After the bridge opened, thousands of people wanted to cross it.*)

3. introduce a surprise or problem. (*Then the problems started!*)

To write strong paragraphs, include these elements:

- **unity:** Describe one main idea, make one argument, or tell one part of a story in one paragraph. When you have a new main idea, begin a new paragraph.

- **cohesion:** Link each sentence to the one that comes before or after. You can use words such as *next, then,* and *however.*

- **organization:** Make sure the sentences are in a logical order.

APPLY

A. Look back and reread the writing model. Underline the first sentence of each paragraph. Discuss these sentences with a partner. What is the purpose of each sentence?

B. Work with a partner. Return to the sentences you underlined in the writing model. Label each sentence *T* (topic), *L* (link), or *S* (surprise) to indicate the purpose of the sentence.

C. Discuss the following questions about the model.

1. What is the main idea of each paragraph?

2. What words or ideas did the writer use to link paragraphs?

3. Did the writer organize the story by time order or by order of importance? How do you know?

Collaborative Writing

A. Read the timeline of the Pearl Bridge in Japan and discuss the events with a partner.

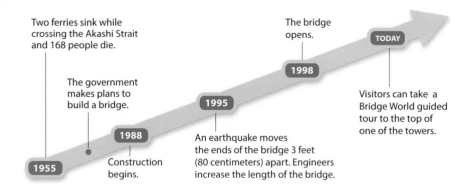

Two ferries sink while crossing the Akashi Strait and 168 people die.

The bridge opens.

TODAY

1998

The government makes plans to build a bridge.

1995

Visitors can take a Bridge World guided tour to the top of one of the towers.

1988

1955

Construction begins.

An earthquake moves the ends of the bridge 3 feet (80 centimeters) apart. Engineers increase the length of the bridge.

B. Do you think these sentences are good first sentences for a paragraph about the Pearl Bridge? Discuss your reasons with a partner. Then work together to write your own first sentence.

1. Y / (N)   The Pearl Bridge is in Japan.

   This is not an interesting sentence. It is just a fact about the bridge.

2. Y / N   In 1995, an earthquake moved the bridge by approximately 3 feet.

3. Y / N   The Japanese constructed the Pearl Bridge after a disaster, but it nearly ended in disaster, too.

4. Y / N   Do you know anything about the Pearl Bridge?

5. Y / N   The Pearl Bridge is one of the most famous and interesting bridges in Japan.

6. Your sentence: _____

   _____

C. With a partner, write a paragraph about the Pearl Bridge. Use information from the timeline in activity A and the facts box. Use this structure to help you.

- description of the bridge
- most surprising fact about the bridge
- history of the bridge
- the bridge today

PEARL BRIDGE FACTS

2.4 miles (4 km) long

towers are nearly 1,000 feet (almost 300 meters) high

6 lanes for traffic

1,737 lights in the cables in red, green, and blue make patterns on national holidays

D. Share your paragraph with another pair. Discuss these questions.

1. Does your paragraph have unity and cohesion?

2. Is the paragraph well-organized?

3. Does the paragraph have a good first sentence?

4. Did you choose appropriate verb tenses?

5. How could you improve your paragraph?

Independent Writing

A. You are going to write a narrative about an architectural structure. It can be a structure you know well, such as your own home, or one you have visited. Brainstorm a list of architectural structures with a partner. Which one do you have the most information about? Choose this structure as the subject of your narrative.

B. Make a timeline of the structure you are going to write about. If you don't know exact dates, put the events in the correct order.

C. Replace the underlined verbs and phrases with stronger verbs from the box below. Two words are extra.

occur	detect	participate
select	~~eliminate~~	research

> **VOCABULARY TIP**
>
> Use a variety of strong, specific verbs (e.g., *construct, detect, occur*) to make narratives more exciting for readers.

eliminate

1. The design for the new bridge will ~~get rid of~~ the old ugly towers.

2. When problems <u>happen</u> with a bridge, the authorities have to close it.

3. You can <u>do some reading about</u> the history of London's bridges.

4. Many people <u>are</u> in the meeting to choose the design for the new bridge.

D. Complete the chart to help you organize your narrative.

Name the structure.	
Describe it.	
Why do you think it is interesting?	
What happened there? Put the events in the correct order.	1. 2. 3.
What is the place like today?	

E. Write your narrative. As you write, use target vocabulary from page 1, use your timeline from activity B to organize your writing, and use a variety of strong, specific verbs to make your writing more interesting.

A. Read your narrative. Answer the questions below, and make revisions as needed.

1. Check (✓) the information you included in your narrative.

   ☐ information about the subject
   ☐ description of the subject
   ☐ description of the setting
   ☐ well-organized paragraphs
   ☐ events in time order

2. Look at the information you did not include. Would adding that information make your narrative more interesting?

Grammar for Editing   Changing Verb Tenses

Don't change verb tense in a paragraph without good reason.

opened
Building began in 1988, and the bridge ~~opens~~ in 1996.

Use simple past, not present perfect, after past time markers.

In 2002, an earthquake ~~has~~ occurred.

Use simple present to describe the situation today.

crosses
The bridge ~~crossed~~ the Thames.

B. Check the language in your narrative. Revise and edit as needed.

Language Checklist
☐ I used target words in my narrative.
☐ I used a variety of strong, specific verbs.
☐ I used simple past and present perfect tenses correctly.

C. Check your narrative again. Repeat activities A and B.

Self-Assessment Review: Go back to page 1 and reassess your knowledge of the target vocabulary. How has your understanding of the words changed? What words do you feel most comfortable using now?

UNIT 2

Getting Your Message

In this unit, you will

> analyze company profiles and learn how they are used in business.
> use descriptive writing.
> increase your understanding of the target academic words for this unit.

WRITING SKILLS

> Audience and Purpose
> Organizing Information
> **GRAMMAR** Adverb Clauses of Time

Self-Assessment

Think about how well you know each target word, and check (✓) the appropriate column. I have…

TARGET WORDS	never seen this word before.	heard or seen the word but am not sure what it means.	heard or seen the word and understand what it means.	used the word confidently in *either* speaking or writing.
AWL				
🔑 commit				
🔑 consult				
🔑 establish				
🔑 exclude				
🔑 expert				
input				
🔑 strategy				
🔑 style				
🔑 target				
transit				
🔑 vehicle				
🔑 vision				

🔑 Oxford 3000™ keywords

Building Knowledge

Read these questions. Discuss your answers in a small group.

1. Why do companies have websites? What can you learn about a company from its website?

2. Name some company websites that you have visited. What features did these websites have in common?

3. What background information should a company have on its website?

Writing Models

A company profile is informational text usually found on the "About Us" page of its website. Read about three different companies.

ABOUT US:
Safari Ads

Since 1998, Safari Ads has **established** itself as the leader in unique[1] advertising. We have built our reputation by designing very unusual advertising **vehicles**. Our vehicles get a lot of
5 attention. How can you ignore a giant truck that looks like a huge cup of your favorite coffee? Our outrageous[2] advertising vehicles will blow you away.[3] Safari has the **expertise** to support your marketing **strategy** and **target** your
10 customers. We work closely with our clients from idea phase until the vehicle is in **transit** from our parking lot.

Here at Safari Ads, our artistic team is our greatest strength. Our master designers and
15 industrial artists have built advertising **vehicles** for major companies in food, fashion, computer,

and sports industries. While we are proud of our designs, we are proudest of our
20 **commitment** to top-notch[4] customer service. That puts us miles ahead of our competition. Take a look at our photos to see what we can do!

---

[1] *unique:* not like others; very unusual
[2] *outrageous:* very strange or unusual; shocking
[3] *blow you away:* impress you or make you very happy
[4] *top-notch:* excellent; of the highest quality

ABOUT US:
Fashion Forward

Are you a fashion-forward person? Then Fashion Forward is the website for you! Started in 2010 by two fashion-crazy friends, Claire Hong and Emily Rose, our website is the fastest, most
5 exciting online shopping experience around. We offer **exclusive** designer dresses, outfits, and accessories at incredible discounts. We feature over 1,000 new **styles** every season, representing 100 designers from 30 different
10 countries. Our merchandise is the highest quality and the most fashion-forward you will find anywhere. Your friends and family will be amazed to see you looking like a million bucks[1] in your **stylish** new clothes from Fashion Forward.

15 Here's how it works. First, you create your own fashion profile on our website. Just take a few

minutes to **input** your height, size, hair color, age, and **style** preferences. Then you will see our fabulous fashions, all custom-selected for
20 you. Explore our website, where you will find designer information, fashion blogs and tips from our fashion **consultants**, and notices about upcoming sales.

Claire and Emily invite you to join them on their
25 search for the latest in what is fashion-forward. They have the **expertise** to bring you the best. Claire, a former model, has an eye for **styles** that can fit anybody and yet be fashionable. With an MBA from the London Business
30 School, Emily knows how to find great prices while providing the best customer service possible. We can't wait to dress you up!

---

[1] *bucks:* informal word for dollars

ABOUT US:
NOM NOM TRUCK

When two young entrepreneurs met at college, they shared a dream: to start a business selling Vietnamese food from a food truck. After college, owners Jennifer Green and Misa Chien
5 recreated their favorite traditional dishes and served them in sandwiches or even tacos from a truck. By 2009, the Nom Nom Truck was **established**. After Jennifer and Misa appeared on a popular food show on national TV, the Nom
10 Nom Truck was on the road to success.

The Nom Nom **vision** is to bring delicious, healthy, and fast Vietnamese cuisine[1] to everyone. Even customers who have never tried

Vietnamese food before love the Nom Nom
15 Truck. After you try our popular Honey Chicken Banh Mi, you will be back for more!

Jennifer and Misa describe their company values as a triangle of happiness. "If our customers are happy and our truck team is
20 happy, then we are happy. We believe in great customer service. We do this by having fantastic, friendly truck teams of chefs and cashiers. Eventually, we would like to have Nom Nom Trucks with Vietnamese cuisine in
25 cities nationwide."

---

[1] *cuisine:* a style of cooking

LEARN

Before you start writing, ask yourself who your readers will be and why they will be reading your text. Consider questions such as these:

- Who is your audience? Do they already know about your topic? If so, don't repeat elementary information. If not, explain basic information and perhaps include examples, diagrams, or pictures.

- How old are your readers? Will they be reading your piece for work (research, perhaps), for business, or for pleasure? Decide whether you should use an informal, conversational style or a more formal tone.

- What is the purpose of your writing? Are you trying to present an opinion, make a recommendation, or interest readers in a product or service?

- Is it important to provide facts or research?

- Do you want your readers to do something? Make specific recommendations or say exactly what they should do, buy, or believe.

APPLY

A. Analyze the audience and purpose of each company profile in the writing model. Write the target audience and purpose for each company. You will use some choices more than once. Compare answers with a partner.

Audience	Purpose
Individuals	Quickly inform the reader
Large companies	Tell a story to interest readers
Advertisers	Communicate what is unique about the company
Women	Make the reader curious
College students	Impress the reader
Online shoppers	
People who live in urban areas	

1. Safari Ads

   Audience: _Large companies,_ _____

   Purpose: _____

2. Fashion Forward

   Audience: _____

   Purpose: _____

3. Nom Nom Truck

   Audience: _____

   Purpose: _____

B. Think about the audience for each of the three businesses. With a partner, discuss these questions for each business.

1. What information might people want when they visit the website?

2. Do you think you are part of the target audience for the site? Why, or why not?

Analyze

A. Reread the three company profiles. Check (✓) the information that is included and mark information that is not included with an X. Which information is included in all three? Compare your answers with a partner.

Type of Information	Safari Ads	Fashion Forward	Nom Nom Truck
Name of owner(s)	X		
Date established			
Brief company history			
Product information			
Statement of mission or vision			
Characteristics of employees			
Description of clients or customers			
Unique features			

B. What is unique about each business? In each profile, underline a few key words that express what is unique and write them below.

1. Safari Ads: _outrageous advertising vehicles_

2. Fashion Forward: _____

3. Nom Nom Truck: _____

C. Discuss these questions with a partner.

1. Which two profiles include information about how the company started? Why do you think this information is included?

2. Does your impression about a company change when you know about the owners?

3. Which profile does not include information about the company's history? Why do you think the company chose not to include that information?

| consult | established | input | style | vehicles |
| strategy | expertise | target | exclusive | transition |

A. Use the target vocabulary to complete the sentences about Two Stamp Design, a website design company.

1. When two brothers ____established____ their website design company five years ago, they knew it was a very competitive business.

2. They focused on developing a very smart long-term _____.

3. They have many years of experience, and they bring their _____ to every project, no matter how small it is.

4. This plan enables them to _____ a wide range of customers.

5. They also _____ with advertising companies and provide advice and recommendations.

6. They hired a photo software expert to provide _____ on their website.

7. Their designs are getting attention because of their sleek _____.

8. Recently, they have designed a website for a(an) _____ luxury resort.

9. They have also completed a website for a company that sells eco-friendly _____.

10. Their _____ from a small company to a recognized business has been slow, but the brothers are happy with their success.

Some verbs *collocate* with, or are often used with, certain other words. These sets of words are called *collocations*. Here are some examples of collocations for the verb *commit* and the noun *commitment*.

The collocation to *make a commitment* means "to make a promise to do something."

> I <u>made a **commitment**</u> to help Tran format the new ad, so I'm very busy at work.

The collocation a *long-term commitment* means "a responsibility over a long period of time."

> Studying to be a nurse requires a <u>long-term **commitment**</u> to a challenging program.

To *commit a crime* means "to do something illegal or bad."

> Job applications often have a question asking if the applicant has **<u>committed a crime</u>**.

To *commit to memory* means "to learn something so that you remember it for a long time."

> Schoolchildren must **commit** the multiplication tables <u>to memory</u>.

To *be committed to* something means "to give time and attention to something that you think is important."

> The company president <u>is **committed** to</u> opening several new stores next year.

CORPUS

B. Answer these questions using the collocations in parentheses. Then share answers with a partner.

1. What responsibilities do you have this weekend? (*make a commitment*)

_____

2. What is an organization or a goal that you are committed to? Explain why it is important to you. (*be committed to*)

_____

3. List two long-term commitments that people often make. Which one have you made or are you likely to make in the future? (*long-term commitment*)

_____

4. What things did you commit to memory when you were in elementary school? What types of things do you have to commit to memory now? (*commit to memory*)

_____

Establish means "to start something" or "to make something exist." *Establish* can be used in several different ways.

A person can *establish* a company, an organization, or a system.

> He **established** his company several years ago.
>
> The government has **established** new guidelines for recycling.

Two people, organizations, or countries can *establish* a relationship, especially a formal one.

> I have **established** contact with the lawyer's office.

You can *establish* yourself or *establish* yourself *as* something; that is, you can succeed in something and make people accept and respect you. A person can also *establish* a reputation for himself or herself.

> He has <u>**established**</u> himself <u>as</u> a very reliable accountant.
>
> She is a well-known opera singer now. She has **established** herself.
>
> The success of her second novel <u>**established**</u> her reputation <u>as</u> an important writer.

CORPUS

C. Discuss these questions with a partner. Then write answers. Use the correct form of *establish* in your answer.

1. Think of the oldest business or company that you know. Approximately when was it established? Who established it? Why?

   _____

2. Think of a famous singer, movie director, or artist. What event (movie, song, or exhibit) helped to establish this person's reputation?

   _____

3. What are some ways that you can establish trust with another person?

   _____

4. How would you like others to see you in the future? In other words, what would you like to establish yourself as?

   _____

The noun *vision* has several different meanings.

It can mean "the ability to see."

> *I have perfect **vision**, so I have never worn glasses.*

Vision can mean "the ability to think about the future with great intelligence."

> *What is needed are good leaders with **vision** and determination.*

Vision can mean "a picture in your imagination."

> *She had **visions** of what her life was going to be and how it was going to turn out.*

CORPUS

D. Answer the questions below.

1. Find the sentence that tells the vision of Nom Nom in the company profile on page 17 and underline it. Which meaning of *vision* is used in that sentence?

   _____

2. Write a sentence that tells the vision of Safari Ads.

   _____

3. Write a sentence that tells the vision of Fashion Forward.

   _____

Grammar | Adverb Clauses of Time

An adverb clause of time indicates when something happened. In a sentence it shows that something happened before, after, or at the same time as an event in the main clause. An adverb clause of time is a dependent clause. It includes a subject and a verb, and it begins with a conjunction such as *while, after, before, as soon as, when, until, soon,* or *after.*

When the dependent clause (underlined below) comes before the main clause, there is a comma between the two clauses.

>   S   V   S   V
> <u>**After the owners appeared on a popular TV show**</u>, the Nom Nom Truck was on the road to success.

When the sentence begins with the main clause, there is no comma.

>   S   V   S   V
> The Nom Nom Truck became very well known <u>*after the owners appeared on a popular TV show*</u>.

In a company profile, the most common verb tenses in adverb clauses of time are simple past, past progressive, simple present, and future.

>   past progressive   simple past
> <u>*While he was attending school*</u>, he opened his first store.

>   simple present   future
> <u>*Once you try our products*</u>, you will see the difference.

A. Read the sentences about Tutor Camp, an after-school tutoring company. Underline the adverb clauses of time. Rewrite each sentence with the adverb clause in a different position.

1. Sam Wilson developed the idea for his company <u>while he was in high school.</u>

   While he was in high school, Sam Wilson developed the idea for his company.

2. As soon as he graduated college in May 2010, he started a small tutoring company for high school students.

   _____

3. Wilson hired a management team after he expanded his business in 2012.

   _____

4. Before he expanded his business, he did a lot of market research.

   _____

5. While he was busy with his company, he was studying in an MBA program.

   _____

B. Read the paragraph. Put brackets around each adverb clause of time, and underline the subject and verb in that clause. Then correct the errors, including verb tense, clause structure, and time words. In some cases, the time word is missing. The first correction is done for you. Correct four more mistakes.

I have always wanted to own my own business, but I wasn't sure what kind.
                    was
[When I ~~am~~ young,] I helped in my father's hair salon. I learned about the

importance of customer service I watched my father talk with his clients.

I also helped him with the accounting while I was a high school student.

When I enter college, I decided to major in business. One semester, just for

something different, I registered in a furniture-making course. After the first

month, I realize that I loved working with wood and designs. I graduated

from college, I started to explore business opportunities in construction

management. I now own my own construction company.

WRITING SKILL — Organizing Information

LEARN

When writing a company profile, you need to capture the reader's attention, give information, and show the reader how your company is special. To do this, decide what information to include, and organize your information carefully.

To plan your writing, follow these steps:

- List three or four main points of information.

- Focus each paragraph on just one or two points.

- Consider the order of the points. You could put the company history first, or it might be more interesting to state the owner's history and goals first.

- Try putting your points in different order. Think about how the order might affect the message and the reader. Remember that a powerful ending can have a lasting effect on readers.

APPLY

Look at the Safari Ads company profile on page 16. Work with a partner to determine the focus or purpose of each paragraph.

Paragraph 1: _____

Paragraph 2: _____

Collaborative Writing

A. The Safari Ads profile does not include information about the founder, the person who started the company. Read about the founder and how he started Safari Ads. As you read, underline key words that describe him or his work.

Nick Alonso, founder of Safari Ads, started his career as an artist and set designer for theaters in New York City. His unusual creations were well-known in the theater world. He designed sets for the top Broadway plays during the 1980s. Later, he took his unique expertise into a new field: designing company exhibits for large conferences. He built extraordinary exhibits around the world. All of this changed, however, when he saw his first advertising vehicle. Suddenly, he had a vision of how he could combine his art with his love of cars. His first advertising vehicle was a cartoon character, which he built with a 1989 Toyota van.

B. With a partner, insert the new information about Nick Alonso into the Safari Ads profile. Follow these steps:

1. Reread the profile on page 16 and decide where the information should go.

2. Rewrite that part of the profile. Use some of the information from the paragraph above, but use your own words.

3. You can write your own first sentence or start with this one:

   Nick Alonso, founder of Safari Ads, is the creative genius behind every one of our unique vehicles.

C. Share your new company profile for Safari Ads with the class. As a class, discuss the questions.

1. Where did you put your new information? Why?

2. How does it change the profile to add information about Nick Alonso?

3. Do you think it is better? Why, or why not?

Independent Writing

A. You are going to write a company profile for a website. It can be for a company that offers a service (such as test preparation tutoring) or a product (such as a clothing store or restaurant). It can be for a real company or a company you make up.

Choose a company. Brainstorm ideas for your company profile. Complete the idea map, and discuss your map with a partner.

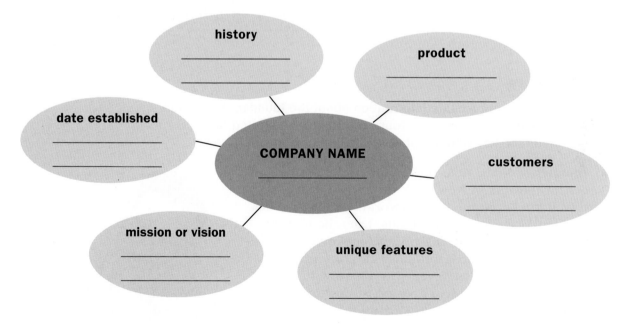

B. For your company profile, include a history of the company. To get ideas, complete the paragraph below with your own words.

The inspiration for _____ came in
                        (company)

a very _____ way. When _____ was _____,
        (adjective)   (person)   (past verb)

_____ realized that _____. With the help
  (person)   (subject + verb)

of _____, _____ established _____ in
   (noun or proper noun)   (person)   (company)

_____. _____ vision for this company is to
   (place)   (person's)

_____.
    (verb)

C. Look at the adjectives from the writing models on pages 16 and 17. Circle the ones you can use in your company profile.

artistic	delicious	exciting	exclusive
fantastic	fashionable	healthy	outrageous
proud	stylish	top-notch	unique

VOCABULARY TIP

Adjectives can help you communicate what is outstanding about your company. Use adjectives in your profile to build the image of your company.

D. Rewrite each of the sentences based on the writing models. Replace the underlined words with information about the company you are going to write about. You may need to make other changes to the sentences as well.

1. Since <u>1998</u>, <u>Safari Ads</u> has established itself as the leader in <u>unique advertising</u>.

   Since 2005, Rumba House has established itself as a leader in teen fashion.

2. Our <u>master designers</u> have <u>built vehicles</u> for <u>major companies</u>.

   _____

3. Our merchandise is the <u>highest quality</u> you will find anywhere.

   _____

4. After you try our <u>popular</u> <u>Honey Chicken Banh Mi</u>, you will be back for more.

   _____

5. At <u>Nom Nom</u>, our vision is to <u>bring delicious Vietnamese cuisine to everyone</u>.

   _____

E. Write your company profile. Use your idea map to decide on the order and focus of your paragraphs. As you write, include adjectives and sentences you like from activities B, C, and D. Use target vocabulary from page 15.

A. Read your company profile. Answer the questions below, and make revisions to your company profile as needed.

1. Check (✓) the information you included in your profile.

   ☐ date company was established   ☐ facts about products

   ☐ name of owner or founder   ☐ descriptions of customers

   ☐ company history   ☐ unique features

   ☐ description of product or service   ☐ statement of vision

2. Look at the information you did not include. Would adding that information make your profile more interesting to customers?

Grammar for Editing   Punctuating Clauses

Compound sentences (with two independent clauses) must have a comma. The comma should be before the coordinating conjunction (*for, and, nor, but, or, yet, so*).

     independent clause   independent clause
Sofia may start a bakery, _or_ she may open a coffee shop.

Sentences starting with an adverb clause of time have a comma after the dependent clause.

adverb time clause   main clause
(dependent)   (independent)
After he graduated, Ray worked in his aunt's business.

When the sentence begins with the main clause, there is no comma.

     main clause   adverb time clause
     (independent)   (dependent)
Ray worked in his aunt's business _after_ he graduated.

B. Check the language in your company profile. Revise and edit as needed.

Language Checklist
☐ I used target words in my profile.
☐ I used descriptive adjectives.
☐ I used adverb clauses of time to tell the company history.
☐ I punctuated my adverb clauses correctly.

C. Check your profile again. Repeat activities A and B.

Self-Assessment Review: Go back to page 15 and reassess your knowledge of the target vocabulary. How has your understanding of the words changed? What words do you feel most comfortable using now?

UNIT 3

Ready for Anything

In this unit, you will

> analyze product reviews and learn how they help consumers make decisions.

> use descriptive and evaluative writing.

> increase your understanding of the target academic words for this unit.

WRITING SKILLS

> Supporting Opinions with Facts

> Writing a Good Title

> **GRAMMAR** Adjectives and Adverbs

$400 to $500 (12)
more
By Rating
★★★★★ (57)
★★★★★ (34)
★★★★★ (17)
★★★★★ (3)
★★★★★ (1)
★★★★★ (2)
★★★★★ (8)

Self-Assessment

Think about how well you know each target word, and check (✓) the appropriate column. I have...

TARGET WORDS	never seen this word before.	heard or seen the word but am not sure what it means.	heard or seen the word and understand what it means.	used the word confidently in *either* speaking or writing.
AWL				
🔑 aspect				
🔑 category				
compatible				
🔑 economy				
equip				
external				
🔑 indicate				
🔑 output				
🔑 overall				
🔑 perspective				
🔑 range				
🔑 technology				

🔑 Oxford 3000™ keywords

Building Knowledge

Read these questions. Discuss your answers in a small group.

1. Have you recently bought something online? Did you read the reviews? Did they help you choose a product? Did you agree with the reviews?

2. What information do you expect to read in a product review?

3. Have you ever written a product review? For what product? What did you write?

Writing Models

A product review gives a customer's opinion about the quality and value of a product. Read these online reviews of three different emergency weather radios.

Great little radio!

ATMOS-FEAR 3000 Weather Radio

★ ★ ★ ★ ★

Finally, a small emergency[1] weather radio that really works! I've owned many radios
5   in this **category**, but they are all terrible compared to the ATMOS-FEAR 3000. A good emergency radio needs to work even if you don't use it for a long time. It also needs to receive radio signals[2] from a wide area. The
10   Atmos-Fear gets it right. It has a solar panel[3] on the top and a flashlight on one end.

It has a hand crank[4] for manual power, or it can run on batteries[5] or an **external** power source. The radio starts easily and charges
15   fast. Its reception[6] is excellent; I can listen to the weather report from anywhere in my house. The display is easy to read, too. The Atmos-Fear 3000 comes with a power **output** for a cell phone, so you can charge your
20   phone if you lose power. The only feature I don't like is the charging **indicator** light. It's too bright, so I don't want it near me at night. Apart from that one small problem, I highly recommend this great little radio.

---

[1] *emergency:* a serious event that needs immediate action
[2] *radio signal:* a radio wave used to send and receive messages
[3] *solar panel:* a flat piece of equipment that uses light and heat energy from the sun to produce electricity or heating
[4] *hand crank:* a bar and handle in the shape of an L that you turn to make electricity
[5] *battery:* a device that provides electricity for a toy, radio, car, etc.
[6] *reception:* the quality of radio signals

You get what you pay for.

PowerUp Emergency Radio

★☆☆☆☆

I was excited to receive this radio because we get many bad storms in our area, and it's important for me to listen to weather
5 news. I have looked at many emergency radios. The PowerUp is much cheaper than similar radios, but unfortunately, this means it is not very good quality. The radio is quite large and is **equipped** with a thermometer, flashlight, and

10 reading light. Sadly, the thermometer was already broken when I opened the box. The lights work well, though. On the one hand, the radio is great because power can come from either a hand crank, batteries, or a solar
15 panel. On the other hand, the hand crank stopped working after one week, and I saw water under the solar panel. Even the radio doesn't work properly. It doesn't have a wide **range**, so it only picks up one very weak
20 signal. **Overall**, the PowerUp Emergency Radio is **economical**, but it's not a good buy. You get what you pay for.

Easy to program, annoying to use.

Red Alert WR50

★★☆☆☆

I bought this radio after I read some online reviews, and I am mostly satisfied with it. The
5 radio has two ways to receive weather information, making it very practical. You can listen to a weather station, or you can receive warnings of dangerous conditions even when your radio is off. The
10 device is **compatible** with a new **technology** for weather radios. This feature means that you only get alerts[1] for your home area, so it won't wake

you up for a storm that's 100 miles away. Sometimes, though, it doesn't work well. It
15 still plays quite a lot of unnecessary alerts. I like that the unit has a memory of 10 past alerts, but I don't like that it doesn't tell you when they occurred. On the other hand, some **aspects** of the radio are very helpful. The
20 display is easy to read, and the radio is easy to program. When the news reports bad weather, a light goes on and a loud sound plays. I like using the Red Alert WR50 **overall**, but I can't recommend it highly. From my
25 **perspective**, it has too many annoying problems.

---

[1] *alert:* a warning of possible danger

LEARN

A good review includes both facts and opinions. A fact is something that is known to be true. A fact can be proven. An opinion, however, is a person's feelings or thoughts about something. Opinions are personal, and other people could disagree with them. In a review, the opinion shows the writer's evaluation: Is the product good or bad?

A good review gives reasons for the writer's evaluations. One way to do this is to use facts to support your opinions.

Opinion

> *The radio is great.*

Opinion supported by facts

> *The radio is great because power can come from either a hand crank, batteries, or a solar panel.*

This will make your writing more persuasive, and your readers will be more likely to trust your recommendations.

When you write a review:

- write an interesting title to summarize your opinion and add a rating (for example, 3 out of 5 stars).

- give your overall opinion about the product.

- describe the product.

- explain why you bought the product (optional).

- give your opinion of the product's strong and weak aspects.

- support your opinions with facts and/or examples.

- conclude with your recommendation.

APPLY

A. Are the following sentences about the three emergency radios facts (*F*) or opinions (*O*)?

_F_ 1. It has a solar panel on the top and a flashlight on one end.

___ 2. The indicator light is too bright.

___ 3. The radio is easy to program.

___ 4. The lights work well.

___ 5. It doesn't have a wide range.

___ 6. It's not a good buy.

___ 7. When a bad storm is reported, a light goes on and a loud sound plays.

___ 8. The device uses a new technology that only plays local alerts.

B. What facts do the reviewers in the writing models use to support these opinions?

1. The ATMOS-FEAR's reception is excellent.

   The reviewer can listen to the weather report from anywhere in the house.

2. The PowerUp is not good quality.

   _____

3. The PowerUp doesn't have good range.

   _____

4. The Red Alert is very practical.

   _____

5. The new technology on the Red Alert does not work well.

   _____

Analyze

A. Why did the reviewers buy these radios? Match the radio to the reason.

____ 1. ATMOS-FEAR 3000

____ 2. PowerUp

____ 3. Red Alert WR50

a. The reviewer read many different reviews and chose this one.

b. The reviewer tried other weather radios first.

c. The reviewer lives in an area with a lot of bad storms.

B. Reread the three reviews and complete the chart.

Aspect / Radio	ATMOS-FEAR	PowerUp	Red Alert WR50
Signal	strong		
Power sources			
Display			
Ease of use			
Other aspects			

C. After reading the reviews, which radio would you buy? Share your answers with a partner.

1. Y / N ATMOS-FEAR 3000 Why? _____

2. Y / N PowerUp Why? _____

3. Y / N Red Alert WR50 Why? _____

Vocabulary Activities | STEP I: Word Level

Word Form Chart			
Noun	**Verb**	**Adjective**	**Adverb**
economy economics	_____	economic economical	economically

A. Complete the sentences with the correct form of the word *economy*.

1. Hybrid cars get excellent fuel _____*economy*_____.

2. It is _____ to buy a large bottle of milk.

3. _____ is the study of money, banks, and markets.

4. Many people lost money in the _____ crisis.

5. Some people buy in large quantities because it is more _____.

6. She was running out of water, so she drank it _____.

When two things or ideas are *compatible*, they go together well.

> *Jim's and Mary's ideas for the school year are* **compatible***.*

When two people are *compatible*, they have similar personalities, or they can live or work well together.

> *My brother and his wife both swim, so they are perfectly* **compatible***.*

We often use *compatible* for two types of technology that work together. Remember to use the preposition *with*.

> *My music player is* **compatible** *with my car radio.*

The opposite of compatible is *incompatible*. It means that two things do not go or work together well or that two people cannot be together happily.

> *These headphones are* **incompatible** *with my music player.*

The noun form of compatible is *compatibility*.

> *Before you buy a new DVD player, check its* **compatibility** *with your TV.*

CORPUS

B. Complete the questions with *compatible*, *incompatible*, or *compatibility*. Then discuss your answers with a partner.

1. Why are you _____ with your best friend?

2. Have you ever bought a(n) _____ piece of technology and returned it to the store?

3. Think of a class you took. Was your way of learning _____ with your teacher's style of teaching?

4. How important is _____ in a friendship?

C. Complete the paragraph with words from the box. You will not use two of the words.

external	output	range	technology
equipped	indicator	aspect	perspective

My MP3 player came (1) _____ with enough space

for thousands of songs and an awesome set of headphones. I

can even connect it to (2) _____ speakers using the

(3) _____ jack. The device is compatible with a wide

(4) _____ of accessories, including cases and covers.

From my (5) _____ there is only one problem with it:

There is a bright red (6) _____ light on the side that

is annoying at night.

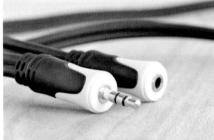

Vocabulary Activities   STEP II: Sentence Level

D. Write sentences to answer these questions. Use a form of the underlined word.

1. What is one of your hobbies? How do you <u>equip</u> yourself for that hobby?

   I enjoy skiing. My equipment includes boots, skis, poles, a hat, and sunglasses.

2. What is an <u>indication</u> that you need to buy new clothes?

   _____

3. How can you <u>categorize</u> your favorite and least favorite foods?

   _____

4. What is a good student <u>equipped</u> with for class?

   _____

5. What do the icons on a computer screen <u>indicate</u>?

   _____

Overall can be an adverb or an adjective. As an adverb, *overall* can mean "generally" or "when you consider everything."

Overall, the radio is very useful.

When used as an adverb, *overall* can also mean "in total."

*We spent three weeks **overall** trying to find the right computer.*

As an adjective, *overall* means "including everything."

*The price of breakfast is part of the **overall** price of the hotel room. High-resolution photos can be printed at almost any size without a real difference in their **overall** quality.*

CORPUS

E. **Put the parts of the sentences in order and rewrite the complete sentence.**

1. many different watches, / but overall / I tried on / I preferred / the blue one

   I tried on many different watches, but overall I preferred the blue one.

2. with this TV, / but overall / there are a few problems / in the store / it is the best one

   _____

3. between family members / cell phones / overall / have improved communication

   _____

4. my overall / is positive / about this computer / opinion

   _____

5. recommend / overall / this new camera / I highly

   _____

F. **Cathy wants a cell phone. Her parents, Abby and Bob, don't think it's a good idea. Abby thinks a cell phone will distract Cathy from her schoolwork. Bob thinks the phone is too expensive.**

1. Write a letter to Abby and Bob from Cathy's perspective. Say why you should have the cell phone. Use forms of all of these words: *technology, equip, aspect, range.*

   Dear Mom and Dad,

   I really need a cell phone because it's essential equipment for a young person.

   _____

   _____

2. What is Bob's perspective? Use forms of all of these words: *perspective, economical, compatible.*

_____

_____

3. Whose perspective do you agree with—Abby's or Bob's? Why? Use forms of all of these words: *overall, aspect, category, indicate.*

_____

_____

Grammar | Adjectives and Adverbs

An adjective is a word that describes a noun. An adjective can appear before a noun or after a linking verb such as *be*.

The Red Alert is a _useful_ radio.   **A weather radio is _useful_.**

You can write more than one adjective for one noun, but it is unusual to write more than two or three adjectives together. Adjectives usually follow this order:

opinion   size   age   shape   color   origin   material   category

a useful red weather radio
a small plastic flashlight

Adverbs describe verbs, adjectives, or whole sentences, but not nouns.

The radio turns on _easily_.

The Red Alert is a _very_ useful radio.

Fortunately, I own a weather radio.

When you write more than one adjective of the same type, such as two opinion adjectives, separate them with commas.

I wanted a cheap, reliable radio.

A. Circle the correct word to complete the sentences in this camera review.

The DX7 is an (1) (*attractive* / *attractively*) digital camera with a

(2) (*square* / *squarely*) black body and an (3) (*unusual* / *unusually*)

comfortable grip. When you press the power button, it opens (4) (*quick* /

quickly). The photos have (5) (*bright* / *brightly*) colors and a (6) (*clear* /

clearly) focus. I even liked using this camera better than my (7) (*great* /

greatly) old film camera. (8) (*Unfortunate* / *Unfortunately*), the DX7 is

(9) (*very* / *real*) expensive, so I cannot recommend it too (10) (*high* / *highly*).

B. Write a sentence using the adjectives in each example.

1. quiet / comfortable

   I can study in a quiet, comfortable place.

2. fast / red

3. expensive / beautiful / new

4. square / small / plastic

5. European / delicious

C. Hiroko and Turki are classmates. Hiroko has just bought a new smartphone. She is comparing it to Turki's older phone. Write a short dialog. Use at least two adjectives or adverbs in each sentence.

   Hiroko: "I just bought a cool new smartphone."
   Turki: "My phone is old, but I can hear very clearly."

WRITING SKILL Writing a Good Title

LEARN

A good title gets the reader's attention, tells the main point, and sometimes gives the writer's opinion or perspective. Writers often draft several titles and then choose the best one.

To write a title for your next paper, choose two or three of these strategies:

- a sentence or phrase from your writing ("I love this little radio")
- a key word, phrase, or idea ("The perfect choice")
- something the reader can hear, see, feel, or taste ("A little red wonder")
- an interesting or unusual idea from the writing ("A radio with a flashlight!")
- a question ("Who needs a radio with a flashlight?")
- a common phrase or saying ("Pump up the volume!")

Follow these guidelines to write your title correctly:

- Avoid very long titles. (Note that titles are not usually complete sentences.)
- In formal papers, capitalize the first letter in every word except short prepositions (*on, at, by*) and articles (*a, an, the*). (This is not always done in product reviews.)
- Always capitalize the first word of the title even if it is a short preposition or article.
- Use the same font as the rest of your paper.
- Center the title.

APPLY

Look at the titles of the three reviews on pages 30–31. Which strategy did the writers use for each title? Do you think they are good titles? Discuss your opinions with a partner.

The title of the first review is a phrase from the last sentence of the review. It's a good title because …

Collaborative Writing

A. Read the following draft of a product review. With a partner, evaluate the draft using the chart below.

My review of a weather radio

The Super Storm weather radio is OK. It is small with a solar panel and crank handle. The radio works well. The flashlight isn't very good. I'm going to send it back and buy a different model.

Aspect	Good	Needs improvement	Missing
1. Title		✓	
2. Description of the product			
3. Opinions about the product			
4. Supporting facts or reasons for the opinions			
5. Recommendation			

B. With a partner, decide how you could improve these aspects of the product review. What could you add or change? Use the information in the writing models to help you.

1. Title _____

2. Description _____

3. Opinions _____

4. Supporting facts/examples _____

5. Recommendation _____

C. Rewrite the review together, including the title. Share your review with another pair. Discuss these questions.

1. Does your review have a good title?

2. Does your review have all the aspects of a good product review?

3. Did you add enough information?

Independent Writing

A. Think of a piece of technology you own that you could write a product review about. It could be a computer, tablet, cell phone, television, watch, calculator, or other device.

Brainstorm both facts and opinions for your product review. Use the chart to help you.

Name of the product:

Type of product:

Description:

Strong aspects	Weak aspects

Recommendation

B. Write three different titles for your review. Use three different techniques from page 39. Ask a classmate to help you choose the best title.

C. Write sentences about your product using the phrases in the Vocabulary Tip box. Give a reason for each opinion. Then choose the one you want for your review.

1. *Overall, I don't fully recommend this TV because the screen is too small.*

2. _____

3. _____

4. _____

D. Write your review. Use the chart in activity A to make sure you include all the aspects of a product review. Support your opinions with facts and examples. Include adjectives and adverbs, and make sure you have a good title and a recommendation.

> **VOCABULARY TIP**
>
> Adverbs can show the strength of your recommendation:
>
> **Strong**
>
> ↑ *highly recommend*
>
> *strongly recommend*
>
> *somewhat recommend*
>
> *don't fully recommend*
>
> *definitely don't recommend*
>
> **Weak**

A. Read your product review. Answer the questions below, and make revisions to your review as needed.

1. Check (✓) the information you included in your review.

   ☐ title   ☐ strong and weak aspects of the product

   ☐ opinion about the product   ☐ facts/examples to support your opinions

   ☐ description of the product   ☐ recommendation

2. Look at the information you did not include. Would adding that information make your review more convincing to a potential customer?

Grammar for Editing   Problems with Adjectives and Adverbs

1. Remember that an adverb can't modify a noun:

   X I needed a cheaply radio.

2. Adjectives don't agree with nouns in English:

   X The radio uses three larges batteries.

3. Notice the difference between the *–ing* and *–ed* form of some adjectives (e.g., *interesting / interested, boring / bored*). The *–ing* form describes the cause of the emotion:

   The camera has an <u>exciting</u> new feature.

   The *–ed* form describes the result:

   I'm <u>excited</u> by this new camera.

B. Check the language in your product review. Revise and edit as needed.

Language Checklist
☐ I used target words in my product review.
☐ I used adjectives and adverbs.
☐ I checked the form of my adjectives and adverbs.
☐ I used adjectives and adverbs correctly.

C. Check your review again. Repeat activities A and B.

Self-Assessment Review: Go back to page 29 and reassess your knowledge of the target vocabulary. How has your understanding of the words changed? What words do you feel most comfortable using now?

UNIT 4

Message in a Book

In this unit, you will

> analyze responses to literature and learn how they are used in academic writing.

> use support for a point of view in writing a response to literature.

> increase your understanding of the target academic words for this unit.

WRITING SKILLS

> Supporting a Point of View
> Summarizing a Story
> GRAMMAR Expressions of Contrast

Self-Assessment

Think about how well you know each target word, and check (✓) the appropriate column. I have...

TARGET WORDS	never seen this word before.	heard or seen the word but am not sure what it means.	heard or seen the word and understand what it means.	used the word confidently in *either* speaking or writing.
AWL				
assess				
🔑 attitude				
🔑 benefit				
🔑 brief				
🔑 context				
contradict				
🔑 devote				
🔑 labor				
margin				
motive				
outcome				
🔑 resolve				

🔑 Oxford 3000™ keywords

Building Knowledge

Read these questions. Discuss your answers in a small group.

1. What are some works of literature you have studied in school? Who are some authors you like?

2. What kinds of assignments have you written in a literature class? Describe them.

3. Folk tales teach a lesson or make an observation about society or human nature. What is a folk tale that you know?

Writing Models

A response to literature is a short summary and an analysis that you write, often in response to an essay question. Read these responses to a test question about a folk tale.

English Literature 101: Mid-term Test

Essay Question:

Read the Middle Eastern folk tale "The Boatman" and write a personal response. What is the message or lesson in the story? Do you agree or disagree with the message? Support your answer
5 with reasons and examples. Begin your response with a **brief** summary of the story. Your response should be no more than 300 words, and it should have proper format with one-inch **margins**.

THE BOATMAN

    A scholar¹ asked a boatman to row him across
10 *the river. The journey was long and slow. The scholar was bored. "Boatman," he called out, "let's have a conversation." Suggesting a topic of special interest to himself, he asked, "Have you ever studied philosophy² or art?"*

    *"No," said the boatman, **laboring** to row the boat. "Subjects like those are of no **benefit** to me."*

15   *"Too bad," said the scholar. "You've wasted half of your life. Such subjects are important for the mind."*

    Later, the boat crashed into a rock in the middle of the river. The boatman turned to the scholar and said, "Tell me, did you ever learn to swim?"

    *"No," said the scholar, "I **devoted** myself to thinking."*

20   *"In that case," said the boatman, "you've wasted all your life. Alas, the boat is sinking."*

---

¹ *scholar:* a person who knows a lot about a subject because he or she has studied it in detail
² *philosophy:* the study of ideas and beliefs about the meaning of life

MAY'S RESPONSE:

The folk tale shows two men with different ideas about what is important in life. The scholar's **attitude** is that intellectual[3] matters, such as philosophy or art, are the most important. The boatman **contradicts** this by pointing out how important practical matters, such as knowing how to swim, are. The scholar feels superior with his
25 knowledge. In the end, the boatman lives longer because he knows how to swim.

I have to agree with the boatman. I can see a similar conflict[4] in the **context** of my own life at the university. Some students **devote** four years of their life to studying a subject like literature or history, and what is the **outcome**? Even though they've worked hard, after they graduate, they can't find a job. However, students who choose a practical
30 field of study, such as business or engineering, can easily enter the world of work. A second example is how students spend their summer breaks. One of my friends says she's tired after the stress of the university, so she just wants to go back to her hometown and stay with her parents. She wants to see her friends again and relax. I understand her **attitude**, but I cannot respect it. I think she should look for a job and get some practical
35 work experience. I have an internship[5] with an accounting firm[6] this summer. Although it isn't a fun job, it is useful. I can earn some money, and I can learn a lot, too. That will help me after I graduate.

Of course, life is not usually a choice between just two things. A person can be practical and still enjoy life. The point is you have to learn the practical subjects before the
40 intellectual ones. Work first, then play. Learn to swim, and then study philosophy and art.

PAOLO'S RESPONSE:

In the Middle Eastern folk tale "The Boatman," two men with different views on life meet on a boat. The scholar feels sorry for the boatman because he has never studied philosophy or art. The boatman, on the other hand, feels sorry for the scholar who has never learned to swim. The boat hits a rock and begins to sink. Not knowing art or
45 philosophy won't kill you, but not knowing how to swim can. The **outcome** of the folk tale is supposed to make us agree with the boatman. He believes that practical matters are more important than intellectual ones.

Before I can **assess** with which man's **attitude** I agree, I have to answer this question: What is important in life? To me, quality is more important than quantity. That
50 means, I want to live well, not just live long. For example, I argued with my parents about my university major. My parents wanted me to study biology so that I could get a medical job. However, I don't enjoy science at all. I don't care how much money doctors or nurses make. I want to have a happy life! So I **resolved** to **devote** myself to literature. When I read novels and poems, I learn about people. I understand their **motives**, their hopes,
55 and their fears. I understand myself better, too. Literature makes me feel joyful. A life with money but without joy doesn't interest me.

My **attitude contradicts** the lesson of the folk tale because I believe we should enjoy life. Life is **brief**. Life is not just eating, sleeping, and working. Life is art and music and creativity and ideas. Even though the boatman will live longer, I believe the scholar lived
60 a fuller and more interesting life.

---

[3] *intellectual:* using or able to use the power of the mind
[4] *conflict:* a fight or an argument
[5] *internship:* a period of time when someone, especially a student, works in order to learn about a particular career
[6] *firm:* a business or company

LEARN

When writing a response to literature, you may be asked to closely analyze a text and give a personal response, relating the text to your ideas and experience. You might write an argument or share your point of view and support it with examples. Your examples can come from your personal experience, from your own knowledge, or from another piece of literature. Strong support for your argument will help your reader understand and possibly agree with your point of view.

When you write a response to literature:

- Carefully read the essay question or test question to help plan your answer.

- Think about your response. What will your answer to the question be? If you could answer in more than one way, choose the way that you can best explain and support.

- Make notes about how you will support your point of view. List examples.

- Make sure that you connect your examples back to the literature.

APPLY

Answer the questions.

1. Reread the essay question on page 44. What must be included in the answer?

2. Look at the summary in each response. Which summary seems more complete? Why?

3. In the writing models, in which paragraph does each student introduce his or her point of view? Underline the sentences.

4. What examples does May use to support her point of view?

5. How does Paolo support his point of view?

Analyze

A. Answer the questions.

1. Which response do you think is better?

   _____

   Which student persuaded you with his or her point of view? List three reasons.

   a. _____

   b. _____

   c. _____

2. What other examples could the writers have used to support their points of view?

   _____

B. With a partner, discuss your answers to activity A. Then answer these questions.

1. Who is the audience for these responses?

2. Why do you think it is acceptable for the writers to use the pronoun *I* in their academic writing?

3. Is there more than one correct answer to the test question? Why, or why not?

Vocabulary Activities STEP I: Word Level

Word Form Chart

Noun	Verb	Adjective	Adverb
benefit	benefit	beneficial	_____
contradiction	contradict	contradictory	_____
margin	_____	marginal	marginally
motive motivation	motivate	motivated unmotivated	_____
resolution	resolve	_____	_____

A. Complete each sentence with the correct word form from the chart.

1. The news reported that the UN _____*resolution*_____ will lead to immediate action in the region.

2. Ana is a(an) _____ student. She works hard and gets good grades.

3. Some insects are very _____ to gardens. For example, ladybugs help by eating harmful insects.

4. Some studies _____ earlier reports that coffee is bad for your health.

5. The new committee will work to discuss recent problems and to _____ some conflicts.

6. My parents gave me _____ advice about my career choice. Each recommended a different career.

7. Studies show that office workers _____ from a daily walk after lunch.

8. When you prepare a written assignment, be sure to follow your instructor's requirements for _____ on the top, bottom, and sides of your paper.

9. Rashid is very intelligent, but he seems to lack _____. He rarely puts much effort into his assignments.

10. My reading speed only _____ improved after I took the speed-reading course. I don't think the course helped me much.

B. Complete the paragraph with words from the box. Use the synonyms in parentheses to help you.

attitude	assessment	brief	context
devote	labors	outcome	

Learner ___Assessment___
(1. Evaluation)

Tran has a very positive _____ toward school and seems to be
(2. behavior)

adapting well to his new first-grade classroom. In the _____
(3. short)

time that he has been in my class, I have observed that he is willing to

_____ himself to classroom activities and work hard. Although
(4. give close attention to)

Tran still _____ with handwritting, he is making progress and
(5. works hard)

writing a little more quickly. He is using his reading skills to guess the

meaning of words in the _____ of the reading. I believe
(6. words that come before or after)

we will see a much-improved _____ in his language and math test
(7. result)

scores by the end of this year.

Vocabulary Activities STEP II: Sentence Level

The verb *assess* has two different meanings.

1. It can mean "to form an opinion about something."
   *The student quickly **assessed** the difficulty of the novel.*

2. It can mean "to guess or decide the value or amount of something."
   *Homeowners might **assess** their home's value at a higher level than a buyer.*
   *The governor said it was too early to **assess** the damage caused by the storm.*

The noun *assessment* refers to the act of judging or deciding the amount of something. Often a noun comes before it: *student assessment, skills assessment, language assessment, damage assessment.*

Next year, the state will use a different <u>student **assessment**</u> *process.*

After the <u>skills **assessment**</u>, *the instructor decided to do several days of review.*

CORPUS

C. Answer the questions about *assessing* and *assessments*. Use a form of *assess* in your answers.

1. If a car is damaged in an accident, who can assess the amount of damage? What is included in the assessment?

   In my country, an insurance company usually asks a mechanic to assess the damage.

   The assessment includes details on the condition of the car and the cost of repairs.

2. What factors does a real estate agent consider to assess the value of a house?

   _____

   _____

3. How does your school assess a student's English language skills?

   _____

   _____

4. In a behavioral assessment, what behaviors and attitudes would a school psychologist assess?

   _____

   _____

5. What does a scientist write up to describe the current state of the lakes, rivers, and forests in a certain area? Why is it important to do this before a building project starts?

   _____

   _____

D. Use the words below and your own ideas to write sentences. You may change the order of the words. Then share your sentences with a partner.

1. at school / assessment / the most challenging

   For me, the most challenging type of assessment at school is a listening test.

2. attitude / toward learning / affect / outcome

   _____

3. chore / labor over / time-consuming

   _____

4. in my opinion / New Year's resolution / every year

   _____

5. hobby / devote / a great deal of time

   _____

Notice the adjectives that are commonly used as collocations with the nouns *attitude*, *benefit*, *outcome*, and *resolution*:

1. *attitude*

   *friendly, positive, responsible, bad, negative, relaxed + **attitude***

   The waiter was very pleasant and had a <u>friendly **attitude**</u>.
   The student's <u>negative **attitude**</u> toward school made it difficult for him to learn.

2. *benefit*

   *great, major, additional, economic, health + **benefit***

   Studies have shown that exercise provides many <u>health **benefits**</u>.

3. *outcome*

   *desirable, good, happy, successful, negative, tragic, unexpected + **outcome***

   The story had a very <u>unexpected **outcome**</u>.

4. *resolution*

   *formal, informal, special, emergency + **resolution***

   After a year of debate, the city council passed a <u>formal **resolution**</u> about street parking.

CORPUS

E. Answer the questions, using collocations with the target words in bold.

1. What types of **benefits** do most large companies offer?

   Large companies offer health and retirement benefits.

2. How would you describe your general **attitude**? Give examples.

3. Describe a recent experience with an unexpected **outcome**.

4. When might a government issue an emergency **resolution**?

5. What are the **benefits** of a university degree?

Although and *even though* can be used in a dependent clause to show contrasting points or ideas. The dependent clause can come before or after the main clause in a sentence. If it comes before, it should be separated from the main clause by a comma. When you write dependent clauses, check for proper punctuation and make sure that each clause has a subject and verb.

                S   V   S   V

<u>Even though</u> they have worked hard, they can't find a job.

           S   V   S V

The internship is a useful job <u>although</u> it isn't fun.

However expresses general contrast. It can come at the beginning, in the middle, or at the end of a sentence. Note how commas are used with *however* depending on where the word is found in the sentence.

<u>However</u>, students who choose a practical area of study can easily enter the world of work.
Students who choose a practical area of study, <u>however</u>, can easily enter the world of work.
Students who choose a practical area of study can easily enter the world of work, <u>however</u>.

The expressions *on the other hand* and *in contrast* express a point that is directly opposite of something mentioned before. These expressions are usually at the beginning or in the middle of a sentence.

The scholar feels sorry for the boatman because he has never studied philosophy or art.
The boatman, <u>on the other hand</u>, feels sorry for the scholar.
<u>In contrast</u>, the boatman feels sorry for the scholar.

A. Combine the two sentences into one sentence, using *although, even though,* or *however.*

1. Aram prepared for the language assessment. He didn't receive a good score.

   Although Aram prepared for the language assessment, he didn't receive a good score.

2. There was a lot of tension at the beginning of the meeting. By the end, the participants were relaxed and laughing.

   _____

3. Li's attitude toward the future was very positive. She had experienced many hardships as a child.

   _____

4. Boris likes to gossip and create controversies. His brother is quiet and keeps to himself.

   _____

5. I saw most of the famous sites in New York City. My visit there was very brief.

   _____

B. Check the following sentences for proper punctuation and correct use of subject and verb. Mark *C* for correct or *X* for incorrect. Correct any errors.

_X_ 1. Although the outcome of the investigation was a surprise. ~~The~~ _, the_ detectives presented a very strong case against the company.

___ 2. I accepted the job offer even though offered me no health benefits.

___ 3. Even though we met several times after our fight we couldn't resolve our differences.

___ 4. Although the economy not very strong, there is quite a bit of new construction in the suburbs.

___ 5. On the other hand, there are several significant disadvantages.

___ 6. She says that she respects my opinions even though contradicts everything I say.

C. Complete the sentences with your own ideas.

1. I like reading poetry. _____Drama_____, on the other hand, isn't ___a type of___ literature I enjoy. _____.

2. I want to learn to play a musical instrument. However, _____ _____.

3. When I was a child, _____. In contrast, I now _____ _____.

4. I want to _____. My friend, however, _____ _____.

5. I might apply for a job overseas. On the other hand, _____ _____.

WRITING SKILL	Summarizing a Story

LEARN

When writing about literature, you may be asked to summarize what you have read. In your summary, include:

- the title.
- the author's name.
- the plot (the main events in the story).
- the outcome.
- a quotation from the story (optional).

Writing a summary demonstrates your understanding of what you just read. By focusing on the key events and the outcome, you can write a clear and concise summary.

1. Before writing your summary, make a few notes about what you plan to include and the order in which you wish to present your ideas.

2. When you write your summary, retell the story using the simple present tense, even though it happened in the past.

3. To retell the story, paraphrase it—that is, tell it in your own words. To do this, try reading the story a few times until you understand it completely. Then put it away and summarize it without looking back at the original.

APPLY

A. Read the summaries at the beginning of each model on page 45. Compare the two summaries by filling in the chart.

Does the summary include ...	May's Response	Paolo's Response
the title? Where?		
characters? Which ones?		
a summary of what happened? Where?		
verbs in the simple present tense?		

Compare your answers to activity A with a partner. Then discuss the following
questions.

1. Why don't the summaries include the folk tale author's name?

2. Which summary is longer?

3. Is one summary better than the other? Why, or why not?

Collaborative Writing

A. Read the Middle Eastern folk tale below. Then discuss with a partner what you
might include in a summary of this story.

The Sack

A wise man came upon an unhappy man
walking along the road to town. "What's
wrong?" asked the wise man.

The unhappy man held up an old sack. "All
that I own in this wide world barely fills
this miserable old sack," he complained.

"That's too bad," said the wise man.
Suddenly, like a thief, he grabbed the sack
from the man's hands and ran down the
road with it.

Having lost everything, the unhappy man
burst into tears. Even more miserable than
before, he continued walking. Meanwhile,
the wise man quickly ran around the bend.
He placed the man's sack in the middle of the
road where he would see it.

Minutes later, when the man saw his bag sitting in the road before him, he
laughed with joy. "My sack! I thought I'd lost you!" he shouted.

Watching through the bushes, the wise man chuckled, "Well, that's one way to
make someone happy! You don't appreciate what you have until you lose it."

B. Complete the chart below with information from "The Sack."

Title	
Characters	
Plot	
Outcome	

C. Compare your chart from activity B with a partner. Then together complete the summary below. Remember to use the simple present.

In the folk tale _____, a(an) _____ meets a(an)

_____ walking along a road. When the unhappy man complains that

_____, the wise man grabs _____.

He places the sack further down the road. When _____,

he is overjoyed. The wise man says, _____.

The lesson in this folk tale is that _____.

Independent Writing

A. Read the essay question about "The Sack." Then complete the following statements to form a response.

Essay question: In the folk tale "The Sack," what is the message for the reader? Do you agree or disagree with the message? State your point of view and support it with reasons and examples. Begin your response with a brief summary of the story.

1. In this folk tale, we see that _____.

2. Although, like the _____ in the story, we often only think of how little we have, the wise man shows that _____.

3. Even though the unhappy man has very little, the wise man wants him to

_____.

4. Looking at my friends, I see many examples of complaining about

_____. Like the unhappy man, some friends _____.

5. I believe that _____.

B. Write your own point of view below. Then add notes about examples that can support your point of view.

Point of view: _____

_____

Example(s): _____

_____

C. Write your response to the essay question. Start with the summary you completed for activity C in Collaborative Writing. You can make changes to the summary if you wish. Then present your point of view and support it with examples.

A. Read your response to literature. Answer the questions below, and make revisions as needed.

1. Check (✓) the information you included in your response.

☐ title of folk tale

☐ characters

☐ summary of the plot in the simple present tense

☐ statement of your point of view

☐ examples to support your point of view

☐ clear connection between examples and the folk tale

2. Look at the information you did not include. Would adding that information make your response more complete?

Grammar for Editing | Punctuating Quotes

When you use a quotation, be sure to punctuate it correctly. If the quotation ends with a period, change it to a comma if the quotation is at the beginning of the sentence.

"Subjects like those are of no benefit to me," says the boatman.
The boatman says, "Subjects like those are of no benefit to me."

If the quotation uses a question mark or exclamation point, don't change it.

The wise man chuckles, "Well, that's one way to make someone happy!"
"What's wrong?" he asks.

B. Check the language in your response. Revise and edit as needed.

Language Checklist
☐ I used target words in my response.
☐ I used the simple present tense to retell the story.
☐ I used expressions of contrast correctly.
☐ I used correct punctuation with quotations.

C. Check your response again. Repeat activities A and B.

Self-Assessment Review: Go back to page 43 and reassess your knowledge of the target vocabulary. How has your understanding of the words changed? What words do you feel most comfortable using now?

UNIT 5

Reporting the Weather

YOUR DAILY FORECAST

World Weather

In this unit, you will

> analyze a news article and learn how it is used to report weather events.
> use descriptive writing.
> increase your understanding of the target academic words for this unit.

WRITING SKILLS

> Selecting Relevant Information
> Using Correct Register
> **GRAMMAR** Quantifiers

Self-Assessment

Think about how well you know each target word, and check (✓) the appropriate column. I have...

TARGET WORDS	never seen this word before.	heard or seen the word but am not sure what it means.	heard or seen the word and understand what it means.	used the word confidently in *either* speaking or writing.
AWL				
🔑 anticipate				
apparent				
automate				
coordinate				
duration				
🔑 network				
ongoing				
🔑 potential				
preliminary				
🔑 priority				
🔑 recover				
🔑 restore				

🔑 Oxford 3000™ keywords

Building Knowledge

Read these questions. Discuss your answers in a small group.

1. How often do you check the weather forecast? Every day? A few times a week?

2. Where do you get information about local weather? Which source has the most reliable and useful information?

3. When you read about weather that has already happened, what information is the most interesting to you? What is the most important?

Writing Model

A news article about the weather describes what has happened or what is predicted to happen and should provide useful information. Read about a severe winter storm from the morning edition of a large city newspaper.

Winter Storm Surprise

Even though yesterday's winter storm didn't break any records, many residents will remember it as the little storm with the big punch.[1] It caught many meteorologists by
5 surprise. "This storm was not on track to hit our area," said Todd Barnes of WBB News. "We didn't **anticipate** more than a few inches of snow. We just didn't see the **potential**. But the winds changed and the temperature dropped
10 last night." After dumping[2] more than a foot of fresh snow in the northern suburbs, the storm has left the area.

Residents of Brooks Street shoveled after a foot of snow fell.

---

[1] *punch:* a hard hit
[2] *dumping:* dropping quickly and in a careless way

Overnight, the city received 10 inches of snow. North Andover received 14 inches.

15 Temperatures dropped to as low as 29 degrees Fahrenheit in some areas, according to the National Weather Service. Winds of up to 15 miles per hour created dangerous driving conditions.

20 Last night on Interstate 90, there was a five-car accident with several serious injuries. **Preliminary** reports indicate that snowy conditions were the cause of the collisions. As of 9 a.m., road crews[3] were still plowing all of 25 the major highways.

"Our **priority** is public safety. Therefore, we are asking people to avoid driving for the **duration** of storm clean-up efforts so that we get the roads safe for travel. There are still 30 **potentially** dangerous conditions. We are **coordinating** our efforts with local and state officials, and snow removal is **ongoing**. However, we expect to make a quick **recovery** from this storm," said State Patrol Officer Conley. 35 He added that public transportation would run on a limited schedule, starting at 1 p.m.

Many areas experienced power outages. The power company estimates about 60,000 customers are still without power. "We are 40 working hard to **restore** power as quickly as possible," said Ms. Gomez of State Electric. She urged residents to stay away from downed power lines[4] and to report them by calling 800-555-6789.

45 School children were delighted, of course. They woke up to an unexpected winter wonderland. Parents across the city received **automated** phone calls late last night about school cancellations. "I'm glad we got the call," 50 said parent Joan Kim. "During the 6 p.m. news, none of the TV **networks** predicted much snow. So I was surprised to get the call a few hours later about school cancellations. But the school administrators made the right decision." Her 55 young boys **apparently** agreed that it was the right decision. They were enjoying the snow as they made a snowman in front of their apartment.

Children went sledding at Wildwood Park.

While most workers are spending the snow 60 day at home, Joe Alonso, a self-employed snowplow driver, was working along Route 2. "I love it when the weather forecasters are wrong," he laughed. "Winter is my business, so I am the happiest when there is a lot of snow."

65 According to the National Weather Service, the weather tomorrow will be clear with no chance of snow. Temperatures will reach a high of 30 degrees Fahrenheit during the day and will fall to 22 degrees Fahrenheit at night. ■

---

[3] *crews:* people working together
[4] *downed power lines:* power lines that fell

Selecting Relevant Information

LEARN

When you write a news article, your goals are to inform readers and to provide useful and interesting information. For a weather article, the information you include will depend on the timing of the weather event itself (for example, if the weather is in the future, if it is ongoing, or if it is in the past). Information will also depend on the severity of the situation. A more serious weather situation will likely require a longer article. You also need to write in a clear and concise style so that readers can easily locate the most important information.

To select relevant information, follow these steps:

- Brainstorm as many ideas and collect as many facts as you can for your article.

- Make sure you include important information such as a description of the weather event, where and when it occurred, what has happened as a result, and whether there are ongoing problems or concerns.

- Check each idea and ask yourself if it is relevant information. Do readers need to know it? Why?

APPLY

The chart below shows information that could be found in a weather article. Reread the writing model. Does it include the following information? If *yes*, list the paragraph number(s). If not, write *no*.

Information in Weather Articles	Yes / No
1. Information from meteorologists or a weather center	*Par. 1, 2, 7*
2. Facts (statistics) about the weather conditions	
3. Road conditions	
4. Accidents caused by weather	
5. Facts about previous storms	
6. Future weather forecast	
7. Health problems that some people may be having	
8. Impact of weather on schools	
9. The writer's feelings and opinion about the storm	
10. Special assistance available to residents	
11. Comparisons to storms in movies	
12. Useful telephone numbers	
13. Reactions and quotations from residents	
14. Comparisons to storms in other areas	

Analyze

A. Think about the audience for the writing model. Discuss the following with a partner.

1. Who is the audience for this news article?

_____

2. Name three pieces of information in the writing model that might be important to that audience.

_____

_____

_____

3. What kind of language is used in the news article? Choose the correct answer.

   a. formal and scientific

   b. informal with idioms and slang

   c. everyday language that is slightly formal

B. Write answers to the following questions, using your answers in the Apply activity.

1. Look at the information in the Apply activity that is not included in the writing model. Why do you think it is not included?

_____

_____

2. What information is given in the first three paragraphs of the writing model? Why is that information given first?

_____

_____

3. The news article is for the morning edition of the paper. What information is important for readers as they make their plans for the day?

_____

_____

C. Compare answers to activity B in a small group. Then discuss these questions.

1. Do you think that paragraph 1 is necessary? Could the writer simply start with the second paragraph? Why, or why not?

2. Find the five quotations in the model and reread them. Why do you think these quotations are included?

3. Why do you think the writer included the fifth and sixth paragraphs? Do you think those paragraphs are important? Why, or why not?

Word Form Chart			
Noun	**Verb**	**Adjective**	**Adverb**
_____	_____	apparent	apparently
_____	automate	automated	_____
coordination coordinator	coordinate	coordinated	_____
_____	_____	potential	potentially
recovery	recover	recoverable	_____

A. Complete each sentence with the correct word form from the chart.

1. By working together, state and local police officers made a ___coordinated___ effort to direct traffic during the power outage.

2. ATM stands for "_____ teller machine." Bank tellers have largely been replaced by these machines.

3. The man on the bus wore a raincoat and carried an umbrella for no _____ reason. It was a warm, sunny day outside.

4. Experts expect _____ from the storm to be quick despite all the damage.

5. The hurricane poses a _____ threat to the coastal areas, so residents should stay tuned for updates on the course of the hurricane.

B. Write *D* for *duration* beside sentences that show a duration of time in the past. Write *O* for *ongoing* beside sentences that show an event that continues into the present.

__D__ 1. There was no rain in Arica, Chile, between October 1903 and January 1918.

____ 2. The Earth's average temperature has risen steadily over the last century.

____ 3. We anticipate continued rains for another three to four days.

____ 4. Japan is still recovering from the tsunami that hit in March 2011.

____ 5. The 160-day heat wave in Marble Bar, Australia, was the longest in history.

The word *priority* can be a noncount noun that means "the most important place among various things that have to be done or among a group of people." Notice the verbs and prepositions it is used with.

The community center <u>gives</u> elderly residents priority.

The operator <u>gives</u> priority <u>to</u> emergency calls.

Disabled passengers <u>take</u> priority <u>over</u> other passengers.

It can also be a count noun that means "something that is most important and should be dealt with first." Notice the verbs it is used with.

If you make your studies a priority, you will be more successful in college.

When planning your college courses, you should identify your priorities.

CORPUS

C. Complete the sentences with a form of *priority* and a verb that collocates with it. Use the correct form of the verb.

1. Improving my physical fitness _____*is*_____ a top _____*priority*_____ for me.

2. Members of the tennis club _____ _____ over

    nonmember players when they sign up for a court.

3. The governor has _____ the employment program a

    _____ for the coming year.

4. In the career workshop, students will complete an exercise to help them

    _____ their _____ .

D. Complete the following paragraph using words from the box.

| anticipate | ~~network~~ | ongoing | potentially | preliminary | priority |

Tonight the top story on the (1) _____*network*_____ news stations is the

wildfire. (2) _____ reports indicate that the fire started in a

campground, although the investigation is (3) _____ . This is a

(4) _____ dangerous situation due to strong winds. Presently,

the (5) _____ is to evacuate residents in the area. "We

(6) _____ that fire crews will work through the night," said

Captain Ramas of the fire department.

Network can mean:

1. a group of people or companies that work together or exchange information.

   *Through sports, Ahmed had developed a large **network** of friends.*

2. a group of TV or radio companies that broadcast the same programs in different parts of a country.

   *Most of the **networks** have a nightly news program.*

3. a complicated system of roads or tracks.

   *The tornado destroyed the **network** of roads around the shopping area.*

4. a system of computers that are connected.

   *The computers in our office are connected to fifty others through a **network**.*

Networking means "a system of trying to meet and talk with people who may be useful to you."

   *People who are very outgoing and sociable are often very good at **networking**.*

The verb *network* means "to try to meet people who may be useful to you in your work" or "to connect a number of computers or devices together."

   *When you are looking for a job, try to **network** with others in your field.*

   *If computers are **networked**, students can read each other's work and make recommendations for revisions.*

CORPUS

E. Rewrite the sentences using a form of *network*.

1. The town has a well-developed system of trains, buses, and subways.

   The town has a well-developed public transportation network.

2. My company recently set up a system to connect all of the computers.

   _____

3. Tomas is skilled at going to business meetings and connecting with people.

   _____

4. Meeting people is a good way to learn about job opportunities.

   _____

5. Emily has many connections in her area of expertise.

   _____

6. All of the major TV stations covered the breaking news about the tornadoes.

   _____

The verb *restore* means "to bring back a situation or feeling that existed before." It can also mean "to repair a building" or "to return a piece of art to its original condition."

*My parents **restored** the front of their house to how it looked 50 years ago.*

The noun *restoration* means "the work of repairing and cleaning an old building or painting."

*The museum is asking for donations for the **restoration** of several old paintings.*

CORPUS

F. Answer the following questions using *restore* or *restoration* in your response. Then compare answers with a partner.

1. What historical building in your town or city needs restoration? Why?

   _____

2. When you are tired or stressed out, what do you do to restore your health?

   _____

3. Everyone occasionally loses confidence in his or her performance at school. How can a person restore confidence?

   _____

Grammar | Quantifiers

When we describe quantities, we can use numbers for count nouns (ten cars) or units of measurement for noncount nouns (two inches of rain). When we want to describe the general quantity or amount of something, we use quantifiers.

Count	Noncount	Either Count or Noncount
many	a great deal of	no
several	much	all
a few of	a little bit of	plenty of
none	a little	a lot of
a couple of		most of
as few as		enough

Count: It caught *many* meterologists by surprise.

Noncount: During the 6 p.m. news, none of the TV networks predicted *much* snow.

Count or noncount: Winter is my business, so I am the happiest when there is *a lot of* snow.

A. Read each sentence. Cross out the one word or phrase that does not complete the sentence correctly. Compare answers with a partner.

1. In my area, we don't receive (*a great deal of / ~~many~~ / much / any*) snow.

2. In the springtime, there is usually (*plenty of / a lot of / a large number of / a great deal of*) wind.

3. We've had (*several / only a few / a large amount of / a few*) storms this winter.

4. Apparently there is (*too much / a few / a lot of / a great deal of*) wind in the area because most of the airport flights are delayed.

5. According to preliminary reports, (*a few inches of / a little / a little bit of / not many*) snow fell overnight.

B. Complete the paragraph with words from the box.

~~large number~~	many of	plenty	several	couple

Los Angeles is suffering through its fifth straight day of unusually high temperatures. The heat wave has forced a (1) __large number__ of residents to stay indoors. (2) _____ the local cooling centers are full of people who have no air conditioning at home. County officials have received (3) _____ reports of senior citizens suffering from heat stroke. In addition, residents are reminded to drink (4) _____ of water and to avoid strenuous outdoor exercise. Meteorologists predict a (5) _____ more days of very high temperature before the heat wave ends.

WRITING SKILL — Using Correct Register

LEARN

In writing, *register* means "the level and style of a piece of writing." Most news articles use a formal register. The writer does not include his or her opinions, comments, or personal stories. The emphasis is on clearly communicating factual information. A news article is usually informative and serious, presenting an objective picture of the news without the writer's opinion or emotion. In a news article:

- use standard English, not overly technical or academic, but not informal.
- avoid the use of slang or abbreviations.
- avoid using personal statements or experiences.
- do not exaggerate or overstate the facts.
- avoid the use of similes (*it was like an oven*) or metaphors (*the city is an oven*).

APPLY

Work with a partner to rewrite these sentences using a formal register. After you finish, compare your answers with the ones in the news article on pages 58–59.

1. It sure caught a bunch of weather guys by surprise! (first paragraph)

   _____

2. Winds like a hurricane created deadly driving conditions. (second paragraph)

   _____

3. My friend said that the cars smashed into each other because the roads had so much snow all over them. (third paragraph)

   _____

4. Lots of places didn't have Internet or lights working and stuff like that... (fourth paragraph)

   _____

5. What I heard was, the weather will be OK tomorrow. (seventh paragraph)

   _____

Collaborative Writing

A. Read the following weather article written for a college blog.

Wow. Yesterday's rain was crazy, wasn't it? In the morning, I thought that I would have to paddle my bike to class. LOL. It was like a flood! Actually, I gave up on my bike and just took the bus instead. Of course, everyone else had the same idea, so on the bus I joined a zillion soaking wet students packed in like sardines in a can. The big surprise is that I made it to class on time. The rain came down in sheets all morning, and traffic was super slow around the campus. One campus bus driver said that Forest Drive was closed due to flooding. Fortunately, Forest Drive is now reopened.

My friend Sam said a big oak tree fell across Circle Drive, and it brought down a power line. Apparently, the wind and rain caused the tree to fall. The result? You guessed it! Students in nearby Stanley Dorm were without power for about six hours. The power company restored power by 7 p.m. Fortunately, there were no injuries reported yesterday. Just buckets of rain! Today we have beautiful sunshine, clear skies, and a freshly washed campus. Weather for the next few days looks fantastic, so get out and enjoy it! A huge picnic, anyone?

B. Work with a partner to answer these questions about the blog article.

1. What register does the writer use—formal or informal? What evidence is there?

2. What are the factual pieces of information? Underline them.

3. What information is overstated or exaggerated? Circle it.

4. What personal stories are included?

5. What idioms, abbreviations, or similes (comparisons with *like*) are included? Circle them.

C. Work together to rewrite the article. Revise it to show a more formal register. In addition, include factual information about the weather found in the box below. You may start the article with the following sentence:

Yesterday's heavy rain caught many students by surprise.

- The rain started at 6:30 a.m.
- According to the campus weather station, two inches of rain fell between 6:30 a.m. and 11:30 a.m.
- The wind averaged about 10 miles per hour, with some gusts up to 15 miles per hour in the afternoon.
- Today's temperatures may reach a high of 75 degrees, with clear skies. The average high for the next few days will be 77 degrees.

Independent Writing

A. Think of a weather event you would like to describe in a news article. It can be an extreme weather event that you experienced, a weather event that you've read about, or something that you imagine.

Brainstorm weather events with a partner. Complete the chart below with extreme weather conditions that are typical for each season. Choose one event to write about.

Fall	Winter	Summer	Spring

B. To plan your article, complete the following chart. Remember, you can use your imagination to create an article.

Description and facts about the weather, including when, where, and how much	
Road conditions, injuries, accidents, or hazards	
Other relevant information (see chart on page 60)	
Reactions and quotations from residents or workers	

C. Write your article. As you write, use target vocabulary from page 57. Use the chart from activity B. Be sure to include appropriate factual information and write in the appropriate register.

REVISE AND EDIT

A. Read your news article. Answer the questions below, and make revisions as needed.

1. Check (✓) the information you included in your article.

   ☐ description of the weather event   ☐ factual information

   ☐ when and where it occurred   ☐ ongoing problems or concerns

   ☐ impact on transportation   ☐ special announcements

2. Look at the information you did not include. Would adding that information make your article more informative?

Grammar for Editing   Using numbers

Use numbers for times and dates. Include *a.m.* or *p.m.* with times.

    6:30 a.m.   March 23

Use numbers for quantities and include the unit of measurement.

    6 inches (6 in.)   27° Celsius (27°C)   100 kilometers per hour (100 kmph)

For numbers of 1,000 and more, include a comma.

    23,000 dollars   2,400 miles   1,000,000 people

B. Check the language in your news article. Revise and edit as needed.

Language Checklist
☐ I used target words in my news article.
☐ I used quantifiers correctly.
☐ I used numbers and units of measurement correctly.

C. Check your article again. Repeat activities A and B.

Self-Assessment Review: Go back to page 57 and reassess your knowledge of the target vocabulary. How has your understanding of the words changed? What words do you feel most comfortable using now?

UNIT 6

Foods of the World

In this unit, you will

> analyze reports and learn how they are used to inform the general public.
> use analytic writing in a report.
> increase your understanding of the target academic words for this unit.

WRITING SKILLS

> Analyzing Ideas
> Organizing Language
> **GRAMMAR** *It is* + adjective + infinitive

Self-Assessment

Think about how well you know each target word, and check (✓) the appropriate column. I have...

TARGET WORDS	never seen this word before.	heard or seen the word but am not sure what it means.	heard or seen the word and understand what it means.	used the word confidently in *either* speaking or writing.
AWL				
🔑 abandon				
🔑 alter				
consume				
diminish				
🔑 domestic				
🔑 impact				
portion				
🔑 proportion				
psychology				
🔑 rely				
🔑 restrict				
🔑 substitute				

🔑 Oxford 3000™ keywords

Building Knowledge

Read these questions. Discuss your answers in a small group.

1. In what ways is your diet healthy? In what ways is it not healthy?

2. What are some typical features of the food from your country or region?

3. What do you know about Japanese food?

Writing Model

An analytic report is a piece of factual writing that explains a complex idea by breaking it into smaller pieces. Read this report about benefits of the Japanese diet.

Benefits of the Japanese Diet

In some ways, Japan is similar to many other developed countries. First of all, the country has a high standard of living. Most people live and work in cities, not on farms. In addition, people
5 are willing to spend a lot of money on food. However, Japan is also unusual. In many other countries, higher incomes have led to increased food **consumption** and then health problems such as obesity[1] and heart disease. In fact,
10 the Japanese enjoy the longest and healthiest lives in the world. Some researchers say this is due to the Japanese diet. Three key aspects of the Japanese diet help make Japan one of the healthiest places on Earth.

WATCH WHAT YOU EAT

15 The first feature of the Japanese diet is the number of calories[2] people eat. The average Japanese person **consumes** approximately 1,000 fewer calories each day than the average American. This has a huge **impact** on

Portion size and presentation are important in a sushi platter.

20 their health because eating less is one of the easiest ways to lose weight. However, Japanese people don't feel **restricted** in their food choices for two reasons:

• **Portion** size: Japanese eat smaller portions
25 at every meal. Research in **psychology** has

---
[1] *obesity:* being extremely overweight
[2] *calorie:* a unit for measuring the energy that a particular amount of food will produce

shown that most people will eat all the food on their plate. Japanese people **diminish** the number of calories they eat by serving small portions of food in individual bowls rather than putting all their food onto one large plate.

- Presentation: Japanese meals are often beautifully presented. Many Japanese parents send their children to school with food cut into artistic shapes, such as vegetables that look like flowers. Children learn to "eat with their eyes." As a result, they eat more slowly and take time to enjoy their meals. This gives their brains time to realize when they are full, so they can stop eating.

FOODS FOR LIFE

Additionally, these three groups of foods help keep the people of Japan healthy:

1. Rice. In Japan, it is a tradition to eat it with every meal, even breakfast. Although white rice is low in fat and contains some protein,[3] it is not especially high in nutritional[4] value. However, rice is filling, so it **restricts** the space in your stomach for other, less healthy foods.
2. Fish. Japan **consumes** a large quantity of fish in **proportion** to the size of its population. Fatty fish like salmon and tuna protect against heart disease. Because fish is their largest source of protein, most Japanese people don't eat much red meat. Eating too much red meat can be bad for a person's heart. But the people of Japan

haven't completely **abandoned** red meat. The Japanese people love to eat a special type of beef called *wagyu*, but they enjoy it in small amounts.

3. Vegetables. The Japanese **rely** on a huge variety of vegetables. One surprising source of vegetables is the sea. Some types of **domestic** seaweed are delicious and healthy because they contain many nutrients and vitamins.

TIME FOR TEA

Finally, the Japanese people drink a lot of green tea. Green tea is important because it contains antioxidants.[5] Research has shown that these antioxidants may reduce blood pressure, lower cholesterol,[6] and help maintain overall good health. Some experts recommend **substituting** green tea for coffee as a healthier alternative. Drinking tea by itself might not **alter** your health greatly, but together with other traditional Japanese foods, it can help you lead a healthier lifestyle.

The Japanese diet has changed over the last 50 years. Today, Japanese people eat more dairy foods, more meat, and less rice. Fast food is popular, along with foreign foods such as bread and pasta. However, Japanese **consumers** still eat healthier than people in most other developed countries. The traditional Japanese diet and eating habits can benefit everyone.

---

[3] *protein:* a substance found in food such as meat, fish, and eggs; it is important for helping people and animals to grow and be healthy

[4] *nutritional:* the way that food affects your health

[5] *antioxidants:* something that removes dangerous substances from the body

[6] *cholesterol:* substance that helps to carry fats inside the body

LEARN

The purpose of some reports is to analyze an idea. That means breaking the idea down into smaller pieces so that the reader can understand each part or aspect. The writing model analyzes the factors that make the Japanese diet healthy and offers support for each idea. The organization of this type of writing moves from general to specific.

- First, break down a big idea into two or three smaller ideas.

- Label the main sections with a heading to explain what each section is about.

- If necessary, subdivide those main sections into smaller parts.

- Visually organize sections by using lists with bullet points (•) or numbers.

- Make sure that each smaller section is developed like a typical paragraph: The topic and main ideas are introduced and then supported with examples or proof.

- If appropriate for your topic, use charts, graphs, and photographs to visually summarize information.

- In the conclusion, summarize the main points from each part so the reader understands the main idea more clearly.

APPLY

A. Read the report again. Complete the diagram to show the writer's analysis of the Japanese diet.

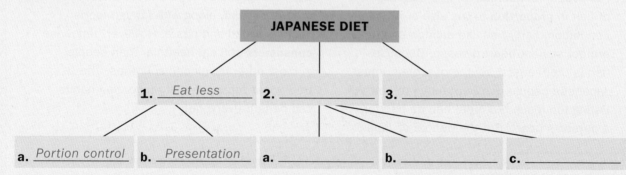

B. The writing model contains several common features of a report. How do these features help you as a reader? Make notes and discuss your ideas with a partner.

1. Headings:

    The headings help me find the main ideas about the Japanese diet.

2. Bullet points and numbered lists:

3. Photographs and captions:

Analyze

A. Discuss these questions with a partner.

1. Who is the audience for this report?

2. Where could you read a report like this?

3. What is the purpose of the report?

B. The report uses several main types of support: research, examples, and cause-effect arguments. Check (✓) the type of support you see in each section. There may be more than one type of support used in each section.

Section	Research	Examples	Cause-Effect Arguments
Introduction	✔	✔	
Watch What You Eat			
Foods for Life			
Time for Tea			
Conclusion			

Vocabulary Activities | STEP I: Word Level

Word Form Chart		
Noun	**Verb**	**Adjective**
alteration	alter	altered alterable alternate unalterable
consumption consumer	consume	_____
reliance reliability	rely	reliable reliant unreliable

A. Choose the correct word form from the box to complete the definitions.

1. A(An) _____consumer_____ is a person who buys something.

2. A(An) _____ car is one that will not break down.

3. _____ is another word for *eat*.

4. If you need to change something, you make a(n) _____.

5. _____ is the act of eating something.

6. Something that you can change is _____.

7. You _____ on people if you need them to help you do something.

8. You work on _____ days if you work Monday, Wednesday, and Friday.

Portion is "a part of something that is shared or part of something larger."
Proportion has a similar meaning: "an amount of something that is part of
a whole." Only *proportion* can mean "a fraction or percentage."

> A **portion** of the money will go to charity.
> The last **portion** of the journey is by bus.
> A large **proportion** of doctors support the new research.
> The **proportion** of fat in people's diets has increased.

Both *portion* and *proportion* have other meanings:

"at the same time"

> The cost of food increases <u>in **proportion** to</u> the cost of oil.

"exaggerated"

> The risk of eating certain foods has been <u>blown out of **proportion**</u>.

"serving size"

> The Japanese eat smaller **portions** of food.

CORPUS

B. **Choose the best word to complete the sentences.**

1. Japanese people eat many (*portions* / *proportions*) of rice a day.

2. The health of Japanese people is in (*portion* / *proportion*) to the way they eat.

3. I only read a small (*portion* / *proportion*) of the book.

4. There should be a higher (*portion* / *proportion*) of vegetables than meat on your plate.

5. The next (*portion* / *proportion*) of the class is about nutrition.

C. **Cross out the word in parentheses that does not have the same meaning.**

1. The benefit of eating vegetables (*diminishes* / *drops* / ~~*increases*~~) if you boil or fry them.

2. The movie had a great (*effect* / *impact* / *difficulty*) on me.

3. This new diet (*limits* / *counts* / *restricts*) the number of calories you can eat.

4. She (*finished* / *abandoned* / *canceled*) the project.

5. We need to (*diminish* / *alter* / *change*) the emphasis in this report to make it more positive.

The adjective *domestic* has several different uses. They all have the basic meaning of "home."

1. *Domestic* describes something that is used in a home.

   *We sell ovens, refrigerators, and other **domestic** appliances.*

2. *Domestic* describes something of or inside a particular country.

   *We sell **domestic** meat and cheese.*

3. A *domestic* person enjoys home life.

   *I'm not very **domestic**. I don't like to cook or clean.*

4. *Domestic* animals are not wild; they are raised by people.

   *Horses and sheep are examples of **domestic** animals.*

CORPUS

D. Write a sentence using *domestic* with these nouns.

1. roommate *My roommate is very domestic. He likes to cook and clean the apartment.*

2. chores

3. chickens

4. airplane flight

5. products

E. Complete the following sentences.

1. It is important to **restrict** _____.

2. It is healthy to **consume** _____.

3. When I need help, I can **rely** on _____.

4. Some people **substitute** tofu for _____.

5. In my country, the **domestic** situation is _____.

F. Answer the questions with complete sentences using the target words in bold.

1. What types of food and drink can have an **impact** on your health?

   Sugary drinks can have a large impact on your health.

2. Do you think people who eat a healthy diet have to **abandon** good food?

3. What can you **substitute** for sugary snacks?

4. Some people get hungry shortly after dinner. How can you **diminish** feelings of hunger at night?

5. Research in **psychology** tells us that people will eat everything on their plate. What other **psychological** research findings about food do you know?

6. What kinds of food do people in your country or region usually **consume**?

7. In your school is the number of teachers in **proportion** to the number of students?

8. Some parents **restrict** their children from eating between meals. Do you agree with this? Why, or why not?

9. Is public transportation **reliable** in your city or town?

10. Do you like to eat at restaurants where the **portions** are large or small?

Grammar *It is* + adjective + infinitive

Use *it is* + adjective + infinitive to describe an action using an adjective.

It is possible to diminish the total number of calories you eat in a day.
It is not necessary to abandon all meat.

Use an infinitive after adjectives of possibility, difficulty, and importance.

Possibility	Difficulty		Importance	
possible	difficult	easy	important	interesting
impossible	hard	safe	necessary	useful

Another way to write these sentences is with a gerund as the subject. For example:

It is + adjective + infinitive	*It is easy to eat* more vegetables.
Gerund	*Eating more vegetables* is easy.
It is + adjective + infinitive	*It is important to learn* about other cultures.
Gerund	*Learning about other cultures* is important.

You can say *whom* an action is easy, difficult, possible, or necessary for:

It is important *for children* to eat vegetables.
Vegetables are important *for children* to eat.

However, be careful not to use the person as the subject:

X *Children are important* to eat vegetables.

A. Write sentences using *it is* + adjective + infinitive (or gerund) and the words below.

1. hard / busy people / eat healthy food

   It is hard for busy people to eat healthy food.

2. easy / buy / low-fat food

   _____

3. important / consumers / read food labels

   _____

4. try new foods / interesting

   _____

5. eat raw fish / not safe / children and the elderly

   _____

B. Complete each sentence with a word or a phrase from the box.

to buy	difficult	important	easy	buying	for consumers

It is (1) ___difficult___ for some people to eat a healthy diet. For example,

(2) _____ fresh food is difficult in some large cities. Sometimes

it is not possible (3) _____ to go to a large supermarket. It is too

expensive (4) _____ fruits and vegetables from small local stores.

As a result, many families have very few choices. It is (5) _____

for them to go to fast-food restaurants or buy prepared foods. It is

(6) _____ to eat a healthy diet, but it can be hard!

C. Answer these questions using *it is* + adjective + infinitive (or gerund) in each answer.

1. Where can you eat at or near your school?

   It is possible to eat at the cafeteria or at a fast-food restaurant.

2. What kind of food can you eat at your school?

   _____

3. Can you buy fresh fruits and vegetables easily near your home now?

   _____

4. What foods are important to eat, in your opinion?

   _____

5. Do you find it interesting to learn about other cultures' food? Why?

   _____

WRITING SKILL Organizing Language

LEARN

Use some or all of these techniques to break an idea into smaller pieces for a report.

Tell the reader how many parts there are.

Three different regions have had an impact on Canadian food.

Write section headings with short phrases that state the topic of the section. Headings function like mini-titles for different sections of your report. They are often written in bold or underlined.

Japanese Food Today

If you use pictures or diagrams, write a caption under each one. Like a title or a heading, a caption does not need to be a complete sentence.

Use bullet points or a numbered list to highlight each subtopic.

- Portion size: Japanese eat smaller portions at every meal.

1. Rice. In Japan, it is a tradition to eat it with every meal, even breakfast.

Use different phrases to introduce each aspect of the main idea. Use phrases like these either in one paragraph or as topic sentences in different paragraphs:

The most important …
The next …
Another …
Finally, …

APPLY

Look again at the writing model on page 72. Underline or highlight all of the organizing language and features. Compare your results with a partner.

Collaborative Writing

A. The diagram below is an analysis of the Mediterranean diet, outlining suggested quantities of certain food groups. Complete the diagram with words from the box.

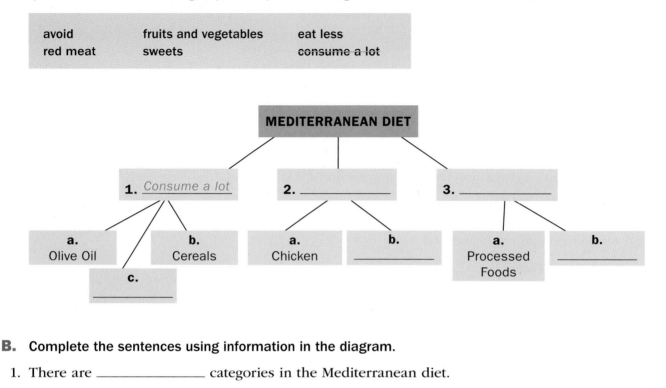

B. Complete the sentences using information in the diagram.

1. There are _____ categories in the Mediterranean diet.

2. You should consume a lot of food from the first group, such as

   _____, _____, and _____.

3. You should restrict your consumption of food in the _____

   category.

4. Challenge yourself to abandon food from the _____ category:

   _____ and _____!

C. Work with a partner. Write a paragraph about the Mediterranean diet using information from the diagram and language from the sentences in activity B.

Independent Writing

A. Make a food diary of everything you consumed during the last three days.

B. Organize your food diary into categories. Write a list of all the foods in each category.

- healthy, unhealthy
- home-cooked, store-bought, restaurant food
- sweet, savory (salty)
- high in calories, low in calories

C. Circle the correct form of the words to complete these sentences. Use a dictionary to check if the nouns are countable or noncountable.

1. I eat a lot of (rice / rices).

2. My diet includes vegetables such as (carrot / carrots).

3. I did not consume a lot of (fish / fishes).

4. There is not much (oil / oils) in my diet.

5. I enjoy making (sandwich / sandwiches).

6. (Noodle / Noodles) are often part of my dinner.

> **VOCABULARY TIP**
>
> Some foods are countable and can be plural: vegetables, sandwiches, or burgers. Other foods are noncountable and must be singular: chicken, rice, tea.

D. Plan your report. Look at the diagrams on pages 74 and 82. Then think about how you want to organize your report. Build your own diagram.

E. Write organizing sentences for your report. Answer these questions to help you.

1. What are the categories in your report? Make a bulleted or numbered list.

2. If you are going to use headings, what will they be?

3. Can you include any useful pictures or diagrams in your report?

F. Write your report. Use organizing language, and structure your report with headings, bullets, and numbered lists. Include some of the target vocabulary from page 71. Pay attention to count and noncount nouns as you write.

REVISE AND EDIT

A. Read your report. Answer the questions below, and make revisions as needed.

1. Check (✓) the information you included in your report.

   ☐ headings
   ☐ bullet points or numbered lists
   ☐ pictures or diagrams with captions
   ☐ a conclusion summarizing your diet or suggesting changes

2. Look at the information you did not include. Would adding that information make your report easier to understand?

Grammar for Editing Gerunds and Infinitives

Gerunds (verb + –*ing*) are used as nouns. Some are subjects:

> *Eating* healthy food is expensive.

Gerunds often follow the verbs *suggest, recommend,* or *enjoy*:

> I <u>suggest</u> *eating* brown rice instead of white rice.

Gerunds also follow adjective + preposition such as *interested in, happy about,* or *afraid of*:

> I'm <u>interested in</u> *learning* about Japanese food.

Infinitives also follow adjectives such as *possible, common,* or *easy*:

> It is <u>possible</u> *to buy* Japanese food in the supermarket.

B. Check the language in your report. Revise and edit as needed.

Language Checklist
☐ I used target words in my report.
☐ I used count and noncount nouns correctly.
☐ I used *It is* + adjective + infinitive (or gerund) correctly.
☐ I used gerunds and infinitives correctly.

C. Check your report again. Repeat activities A and B.

Self-Assessment Review: Go back to page 71 and reassess your knowledge of the target vocabulary. How has your understanding of the words changed? What words do you feel most comfortable using now?

UNIT 7

Heat + Pressure = Diamonds

In this unit, you will

> analyze responses to essay test questions and learn how they are used in geology and other sciences.
> use a causal explanation to describe a process.
> increase your understanding of the target academic words for this unit.

WRITING SKILLS

> Analyzing a Causal Explanation
> Responding to a Test Question
> GRAMMAR Present Passive Voice

Self-Assessment

Think about how well you know each target word, and check (✓) the appropriate column. I have…

TARGET WORDS	never seen this word before.	heard or seen the word but am not sure what it means.	heard or seen the word and understand what it means.	used the word confidently in *either* speaking or writing.
AWL				
🔑 create				
currency				
🔑 drama				
🔑 enable				
insert				
intermediate				
🔑 principal				
🔑 proceed				
🔑 shift				
🔑 structure				
🔑 unique				
visual				

🔑 Oxford 3000™ keywords

Building Knowledge

Read these questions. Discuss your answers in a small group.

1. Describe a diamond. What are some of its characteristics?

2. Where do diamonds come from?

3. What kind of information would you expect to find in an explanation about diamonds?

Writing Model

A causal explanation is a piece of writing that tells how and why something happens. Read a student's causal explanation in an answer to a geology class test question.

Introduction to Geology

Test Question: Diamonds are highly valued gems in every **currency** around the world. Explain what a diamond is, its **unique** characteristics, how it is formed, and what it is used for. Label the parts of the attached illustration with words from the box.

diamond crystals	Earth's surface	hardened magma rock
hot magma	mantle	pipe

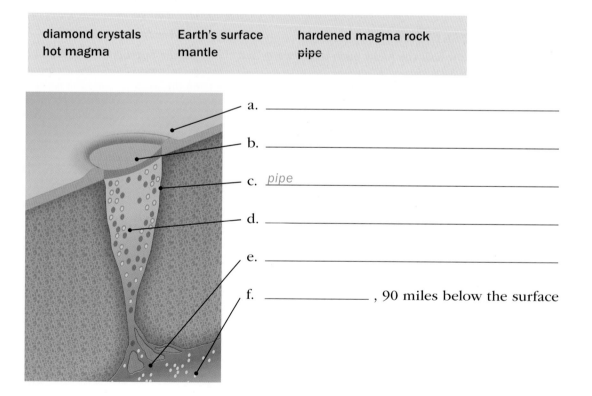

a. _____

b. _____

c. _pipe_ _____

d. _____

e. _____

f. _____, 90 miles below the surface

A diamond is a crystal of pure carbon. Carbon is a chemical element that exists in all living things. Graphite, the soft material in a lead pencil, is made of pure carbon. But when a single carbon atom[1] connects with four other carbon atoms, it forms an incredibly strong crystal. A diamond is the world's hardest natural material, partly due to this pure carbon **structure**. A diamond is so hard that it can only be cut by another diamond. Diamonds can withstand extremely high and low temperatures, so they are used in computers and scientific equipment. When diamonds are cut and polished for jewelry, the crystals are **visually** stunning.[2]

Although diamonds are **principally** used for jewelry, their use has **shifted** to other areas. Because of their extreme durability, diamonds now have many industrial uses. For example, diamonds are now **inserted** into surgical tools, tiny medical devices, and computer microchips. In short, their value now extends beyond jewelry to many industrial applications.

Diamonds form deep under the surface of the Earth. The process can take millions of years, so the diamonds we see today are extremely old. Diamonds are formed in the mantle, an area about 90 miles (150 kilometers) below the Earth's surface. Temperatures in the mantle reach at least 2,000 degrees Fahrenheit (1,050 degrees Celsius). There is also a great deal of pressure because heavy rocks on the Earth's surface press down on the mantle. The extreme heat and pressure change pure carbon into diamond crystals. At this **intermediate** stage, the diamond crystals are over 90 miles beneath the surface. They are unreachable. However, nature brings them to the surface in a very **dramatic** way.

Violent volcanic eruptions[3] are the key. These explosions carry some carbon crystals to the surface of the Earth. During these eruptions, hot magma, or hot liquid rock, pushes the diamonds from the mantle to the surface. The eruptions carry the diamonds very quickly, **proceeding** upward in just a few hours. When this happens, the diamonds come from an extremely hot environment up to the Earth's cooler surface. There, the diamonds cool quickly, and as a result, the carbon atoms stay locked in a crystal **structure**. The volcanic magma cools and hardens. These eruptions **create** pipes, or carrot-shaped openings in the Earth. The pipes are lined with hardened magma rock. The pipes usually extend to about 2.5 kilometers below the Earth's surface. Slowly, upper levels of the pipes are eroded,[4] and this exposes the diamonds. This is how diamond areas are discovered.

Today, most natural diamonds come from mines[5] in Africa, Canada, Russia, and Australia. There, diamonds are mined deep in the pipes below the Earth's surface. Diamonds are also found in sediment[6] near rivers or along a coast. These sources are in Asia and South America. However, mining diamonds is an expensive and dangerous business. As the uses and demand for diamonds have grown, scientists have developed and perfected the manufacture of synthetic[7] diamonds. The greater availability and lower cost of synthetic diamonds have **enabled** scientists to explore new ways to use diamonds in industry.

---

[1] *atom:* the smallest part into which a chemical element can be divided
[2] *stunning:* very attractive or impressive
[3] *volcanic eruptions:* explosions of fire, smoke, and rock that has melted
[4] *be eroded:* be destroyed or worn away by natural forces, such as wind and water
[5] *mines:* a system of holes that people dig underground in order to obtain natural resources
[6] *sediment:* thick substance that forms at the bottom of a liquid
[7] *synthetic:* made by a chemical process; not natural

LEARN

When you are asked to explain *how* something is formed or takes place, you are writing a causal explanation. A causal explanation usually includes both a cause (reason) and some effects (results). When you can explain how something happens, you show your understand of the process.

Use the following language to signal causes and effects.

Cause: floods   Effect: water erodes riverbanks

- The cause can be in a dependent clause with *because, since,* or *when.*

  When there are floods, water erodes riverbanks.

- A cause can also be stated with *because of* or *due to.*

  The riverbanks have eroded due to flooding.

- The result can be introduced by *so, resulting in,* or *causing.*

  There were many floods this spring, so the riverbank has eroded.

  There were heavy rains, resulting in erosion.

APPLY

A. Reread the first paragraph in the writing model. Circle the words and phrases that signal a cause-effect relationship.

B. Match each cause from the paragraph to its effect.

Causes

___d___ 1. one carbon atom joins four other carbon atoms

_____ 2. diamonds have a pure carbon structure

_____ 3. diamonds can resist heat and cold

_____ 4. jewelers cut and polish diamonds

_____ 5. a diamond is very hard

Effects

a. only a diamond can cut another diamond

b. they are extremely hard

c. they look very beautiful

d. a very strong crystal forms

e. computers and scientific machines use them

C. Write complete sentences from the causes and effects in activity B. Use the language from Learn above to show cause and effect.

_____

_____

_____

Analyze

A. What topics are covered in the writing model? If the topic is included, list the paragraph where it is found. Write an X if the topic is not included.

_____ a. uses for diamonds   _____ d. how synthetic diamonds are made

_____ b. cost of diamonds   _____ e. where diamonds are mined

_____ c. definition of a diamond   _____ f. characteristics of diamonds

B. Use information in the writing model to label the diagram on page 86. Then check your answers with a partner.

C. Answer the following questions about cause-effect relationships in the third and fourth paragraphs.

1. What is one factor that creates pressure in the mantle?

_____

2. What causes pure carbon to change into diamond crystals?

_____

3. Why are diamonds unreachable in the mantle?

_____

4. What causes carbon atoms to become locked into a crystal structure?

_____

5. How does erosion expose diamonds in the pipes?

_____

D. Work with a partner to complete the following.

1. For each of the following subjects, write a specific topic that could include a causal explanation.

a. Geology: _how a canyon forms_____

b. Biology: _____

c. Environmental studies: _____

d. History: _____

2. In what classes have you had to write a causal explanation? What was the assignment?

_____

_____

_____

Here are some common collocations for *enable, insert, proceed, shift, visualize,* and *intermediate.*

1. *enable* someone to view / reach / discover / access something

   Today's technology **enables** companies <u>to reach</u> customers in many new ways.

2. *insert* a card / a key / a needle / a page / a comment

   When I revised my paper, I **inserted** <u>a page</u> of additional background information.

3. promise to / intend to / wish to / decide to *proceed*

   Even though it was raining, they <u>decided to **proceed**</u> with the parade.

4. *shift* constantly / gradually / quickly

   The weather pattern has **shifted** <u>gradually</u> in the last few days.

5. be able to / be difficult to / be easy to / try to *visualize*

   It's <u>difficult to **visualize**</u> what this area looked like many centuries ago.

6. an *intermediate* step / stage / level / class

   Many countries issue new drivers a learner's permit as an **intermediate** <u>stage</u> before they get a driver's license.

CORPUS

A. **Use collocations from the corpus box to complete the following sentences. Use the correct form of the verb.**

1. When someone gives me verbal directions to a location, I <u> try to visualize </u> the information in my mind.

2. A scholarship will _____ my brother _____ his goal of attending graduate school.

3. As he was standing in front of the class, the shy boy _____ from foot to foot.

4. When I _____ my bank card into the ATM outside of my bank, the machine froze and showed an error message.

5. Congratulations! You passed the beginner level! You're now ready for the

   _____.

6. Even though the research team didn't receive as much money as they had requested, they _____ with the experiment anyway.

Word Form Chart

Noun	Verb	Adjective	Adverb
drama	_____	dramatic	dramatically
principal	_____	principal	principally
structure	structure	structural	structurally
uniqueness	_____	unique	uniquely

B. Complete each sentence with the correct word form from the chart.

1. The school _____*principal*_____ introduced the guest speaker, a geologist, to the students.

2. There was a _____ difference between the coastline before and after the historic hurricane.

3. Ahmed is studying to be a _____ engineer. He is especially interested in bridges.

4. The _____ reason for the meeting was to plan the new environmental study.

5. The report is _____ concerned with the effects of winter weather on traffic patterns.

6. Tonight is the opening night of a new _____ about life during the 1960s.

7. Each natural diamond is _____. No two are alike.

The word *principal* can be a noun or an adjective. As a noun, it means "the person who is in charge of a school." As an adjective, it means "most important" or "main."

> Our high school **principal** is retiring next year.

> The release of pressure inside the earth is a **principal** cause of earthquakes.

Don't confuse the nouns *principal* and *principle*. *Principle* means "a basic or general rule or truth" or "a law of science."

> The system works on the **principle** that heat rises.

CORPUS

C. Complete the sentences with a form of *principal* or *principle*.

1. The _____*principal*_____ actors in the play were not well known.

2. My father had high _____ about how to conduct business.

3. The _____ investigator at the crime scene was feeling sick.

4. The school is very large, so it has one _____ and two vice _____.

5. It is against my _____ to steal even the smallest item.

6. A fundamental _____ of geology is that newer rocks are laid down on top of older rocks, forming layers of rock.

Vocabulary Activities | STEP II: Sentence Level

D. Answer the following questions with a partner. Use *currency* or *currencies* in your answer.

1. How many different foreign currencies can you name?

_____

2. What currency is used in many European countries?

_____

3. Where can you exchange foreign currency?

_____

1. The verb *create* can mean "to make something new or original" or "to produce a particular feeling or impression."

   *Our company is working to **create** a smaller, lighter printer.*
   *Candles at the dinner table **created** a romantic atmosphere.*

2. The noun *creativity* often combines with these words:

   artistic creativity   encourage creativity   inhibit creativity

   *Criticizing a child too much can <u>inhibit **creativity**</u>. Children need to experiment and make mistakes, too.*

   CORPUS

E. Write answers to the following questions. Then share your answers with a partner.

1. Do you know someone with a great deal of artistic creativity? Describe the person's art and how it shows creativity.

_____

2. How can working in a group encourage or inhibit creativity?

_____

3. What companies are creating useful or interesting products?

_____

4. How can a coffee shop owner create a welcoming atmosphere?

_____

5. In what ways are you creative?

_____

Grammar | Present Passive Voice

Transitive verbs are verbs that require a direct object. Transitive verbs have active and passive forms. In a passive sentence, the subject is not the doer of the action. Often, information about who does the action is *not included*.

Diamonds _are polished_ and then they _are made_ into jewelry.

We use the present passive voice to explain how something is done or how something happens. A passive sentence focuses on the person or thing that receives the action.

Compare these examples.

1. Active (the subject is doing the action)

    The scientist _inserts_ the slide into the microscope.

2. Passive (the subject receives the action)

    The slide _is inserted_ into the microscope.

3. Passive (the agent is mentioned with by)

    The slide _is inserted_ by the scientist.

To form the passive voice in the present, use the correct form of *be* + past participle of the verb.

Currency _is exchanged_ in a bank.

The passive voice is very useful in describing a process or how something is done. Use the passive voice when the subject of the verb is not known or is not important.

A. Complete the following sentences with passive voice. Find the passive forms of the verbs in the writing model on pages 86–87.

1. Diamonds _____*are used*_____ in computers and scientific equipment.

2. Diamonds _____ and _____ for jewelry.

3. Diamonds _____ now _____ into surgical tools, tiny medical devices, and computer microchips.

4. Diamonds _____ in the mantle.

5. The pipes _____ with hardened magma rock.

6. Diamond areas _____ below the Earth's surface.

7. Diamonds _____ also _____ in sediment near rivers or along a coast.

B. Complete the paragraph. Use the correct form of the verb in the passive voice.

Wood _is transformed_ into petrified wood in a process that takes thousands
        (1. transform)

of years. It starts when a tree falls down. The tree _____ away
                                                          (2. carry)

by a river. Eventually, the tree _____ in layer upon layer of mud.
                                      (3. bury)

There is no oxygen, so the tree doesn't rot or decompose. Instead, the tree

structure slowly breaks down. Over time, the small spaces inside the tree

_____ with mineral crystals. In the end, the entire tree becomes
    (4. fill)

like a rock. Petrified wood can be of many different colors, depending on the

minerals. Petrified wood _____ in many countries.
                              (5. find)

Petrified wood can be very colorful.

C. Rewrite the following active sentences in the passive voice.

1. Students study rocks under a microscope.

   Rocks are studied under a microscope.

2. People do not usually use gold for a currency.

   _____

3. Workers mine coal either in open pits or underground.

   _____

4. People use coal for energy or to generate electricity.

   _____

WRITING SKILL · Responding to a Test Question

LEARN

Some tests require you to write an explanation to demonstrate your knowledge about a topic. You might start your explanation with a definition of the term or concept. You may describe some characteristics or unique attributes. Then you will explain how something is formed or how it takes place. Some test questions ask you to write an answer of one or more paragraphs. Keep these tips in mind to answer a test question effectively:

- Read the question carefully to see exactly what must be included in your answer. Do you need to include a definition? Do you need to explain more than one process? Underline the key points in the test question.

- Think about how much time you have to answer the question and consider how many paragraphs you may need to write. Manage your time carefully. Allow time to plan your answer, write your answer, and read over your answer before you hand it in.

- Make a quick rough outline of the key points you will cover in your answer. Then reread the question again to make sure you will directly answer it.

- Keep your answer direct and to the point. Demonstrate your knowledge of the topic, but stick to the questions. You don't need to include everything that you know about the topic.

APPLY

Look at the writing model and response on pages 86–87. Discuss the questions with a partner.

1. How many different things must be included in the response? What are they?

   _____

   _____

2. Did the writer include everything required? If not, what was missing?

   _____

3. Imagine the writer had 40 minutes to answer the question. How would you recommend the writer spend that time?

   _____

   _____

Collaborative Writing

A. **With a partner, review and discuss the student notes below. Then answer the questions about the process.**

1. Which method is explained in the notes?

2. What three things are placed in the container?

3. What causes the graphite to separate into individual atoms?

4. How long does the procedure take?

5. Why isn't the synthetic diamond as pure as a natural diamond?

"Diamond" comes from a Greek word meaning "unbreakable." Diamonds are very hard. They transfer heat better than any metal.

First synthetic diamond was created in 1954. The process wasn't perfected until 1990s.

Most common way to create synthetic diamonds— high pressure, high temperature (HPHT)

Pressure

Heater

Container with seed, graphite, solution

Pressure

- *scientists start with seed—tiny diamond, the size of a period*
- *in special container, seed is placed with graphite (pure carbon) + special liquid solution*
- *container is closed, then is placed under intense heat and pressure*
- *pressure enables graphite (pure carbon) to separate into individual atoms*
- *atoms attach to the diamond seed and grow*
- *procedure takes only a few days*

Synthetic—not as pure or attractive as a natural diamond due to metals in solution. Can make different colors, but can't make very big diamonds. Less expensive than natural ones.
Diamonds are cut. Used for jewelry or for high-tech medical instruments.

B. **Read the test question. Underline key words that tell what to include in your answer.**

Test Question: Explain one method for manufacturing synthetic diamonds. Include information on how synthetic diamonds compare with natural ones and what synthetic diamonds are primarily used for.

C. **Review the student notes in activity A and plan your answer to the test question.**

1. Discuss what information in the notes you would not include, and give reasons. Mark with an X the information you will not include.

2. Plan your answer by completing the rough outline below.

A. Steps in a method: _____

_____

_____

B. How synthetic diamonds compare to real diamonds:

_____

C. Uses: _____

D. Work with a partner or in a small group to write an answer to the test question.

Independent Writing

A. Read the test question. Number the three topics you need to include in a response to the question. Then read the notes below.

Test question: Explain what a synthetic diamond is. Describe its characteristics, and tell how it is made.

> *Synthetic diamond: human-made reproduction; same chemical composition, crystal structure, and physical characteristics as a natural diamond.*
> - *Great demand for synthetic diamonds, especially for high-tech industries*
> - *Plays a key role in industries such as mining, construction, and electronics Also used for machine tools, cutting tools*
> - *Can be made to the exact size needed in industry*
> - *95 percent of diamonds used in industry are synthetic*
> - *Synthetics are flawless. Since flaws affect hardness, synthetics are harder than natural diamonds. Better in tools.*
> - *Hard to visually distinguish synthetic from natural diamonds*
> - *Cheaper by 30 percent*
> - *More pure—natural diamonds may have small imperfections*
> - *Unique colors of natural diamonds can't be reproduced, but synthetic ones are available in blue, pink, white, yellow, and orange*
> - *Unlike natural diamonds, contain some metals—otherwise, exactly the same*
> - *Synthetic diamonds not as large as natural ones, so not as good for jewelry*

B. Organize your ideas in a rough outline similar to the one used in activity C above.

C. Write your answer to the test question. Use your outline to organize your response. Make sure you answer the question directly and only include the information that is required. Include target vocabulary in your response.

A. Read your test response. Answer the questions below, and make revisions as needed.

1. Check (✓) the information you included in your test response.

☐ definition   ☐ steps in the manufacturing process

☐ unique characteristics   ☐ causal explanations

☐ uses   ☐ comparisons with natural diamonds

2. Look at the information you did not include. Would adding that information make your test response clearer?

Grammar for Editing | Irregular Verbs

When you use the present passive voice, make sure that you spell the past participle correctly. Be especially careful with irregular verb forms.

Verb	Past Participle	Example
find	found	Petrified wood is found in some deserts.
catch	caught	Leaves are caught in the mud.
buy	bought	Equipment is bought with funds from the government.
make	made	Synthetic diamonds are made in laboratories.
build	built	High fences are built to keep animals out.
take	taken	Photographs are taken of the same place every year.

B. Check the language in your test response. Revise and edit as needed.

Language Checklist
☐ I used target words in my test response.
☐ I used language for causal explanations.
☐ I used the present passive voice correctly.
☐ I used irregular verb forms in the present passive correctly.

C. Check your test response again. Repeat activities A and B.

Self-Assessment Review: Go back to page 85 and reassess your knowledge of the target vocabulary. How has your understanding of the words changed? What words do you feel most comfortable using now?

UNIT 8

The Wireless Classroom

In this unit, you will

> analyze anecdotes and learn how they are used in discussion board posts.
> use anecdotes in persuasive writing.
> increase your understanding of the target academic words for this unit.

WRITING SKILLS

> Anecdotes
> Writing a Thesis
> GRAMMAR Modals

Self-Assessment

Think about how well you know each target word, and check (✓) the appropriate column. I have...

TARGET WORDS	never seen this word before.	heard or seen the word but am not sure what it means.	heard or seen the word and understand what it means.	used the word confidently in *either* speaking or writing.
AWL				
academy				
⚷ cease				
⚷ estimate				
evolve				
⚷ generation				
integrity				
mature				
⚷ policy				
reluctance				
rigid				
scenario				
⚷ survive				

⚷ Oxford 3000™ keywords

Building Knowledge

Read these questions. Discuss your answers in a small group.

1. Can you use cell phones, laptops, or tablet computers in your classes?

2. Do you think technology improves learning?

3. What is an online discussion board? Why might you use one in a class?

Writing Models

A class discussion board post is a comment made in an online conversation among students and sometimes the teacher. Read two responses to a professor's question by university students in the same class.

SHOULD CELL PHONE USE BE ALLOWED IN THE CLASSROOM?

15 COMMENTS

NEWEST ▼   WRITE A COMMENT

Annie

I used to think that cell phones were a distraction[1] in class. Now, however, I believe that students and teachers should be able to use them. Cell phones can actually help out in the classroom. I changed my mind because of two experiences I had in Dr. Biedermeier's composition
5   class last semester.

The first time was at the end of the first lesson when the professor wrote the homework assignment on the board. My classmate picked up his smartphone and took a photo of the board. I expected Professor Biedermeier to be angry at the student for breaking the school's cell
10   phone **policy**. Instead, he was pleased because the photograph could accurately record the homework. He even encourged my classmate to email the picture to everyone else!

In the next class, Dr. Biedermeier assigned our first writing task. We had to write a letter to the school newspaper arguing for or against the
15   construction of a new sports stadium on campus. When we finished our first draft, we had to record ourselves reading our essay using our cell

---

[1] *distraction:* something that takes your attention away from what you were doing or thinking about

phones or laptops. I was **reluctant** at first because I didn't like to hear myself reading out loud. However, I was amazed because I heard some of my own mistakes! I **estimated** that I caught half of my grammar mistakes that way. I even found that my argument wasn't strong enough, so I revised it before the professor read it.

I didn't expect my cell phone to make me a better writer, but after this experience, I use recordings in almost all my classes. I don't think that teachers should have a **rigid** policy about technology. Cell phones can be good or bad in the classroom. I think most students are **mature** enough to know when to use them.

POSTED MONDAY, 4:35 P.M.

Bill

I'm not a technophobe,[1] and I realize technology has **evolved**, but I think cell phones should be restricted in the classroom. I have no problem with students who use their phones to take notes or record lectures. However, too many students are glued to their screens, paying no attention for the duration of class.

Yesterday in my history class, the professor was leading an interesting discussion. However, half the students had their heads down and their fingers on their smartphones. This is a common **scenario** in almost every class. Many of my classmates read email, check social media sites, or even play online games. Why do they bother to come to class? One classmate told me that she couldn't **survive** 50 minutes without being in contact with her friends. She said she might miss an important message or not know the latest gossip[2] if she **ceased** her cell phone use in class. But she can't learn if she's always thinking about something else. Even worse, I have friends who write **academic** papers using text message abbreviations.[3] Teachers should require all students to speak and write in formal English. Some of my friends can't have a normal conversation because they spend more time looking at their phones than at real people. If we can't use cell phones in class, then we'll have to talk face-to-face, and that's better for everyone.

Schools have a responsibility to teach our **generation** how to unplug, concentrate, and make human contact. Restricting the use of digital devices to educational purposes such as note-taking might improve the **integrity** of class discussions.

POSTED TUESDAY, 8:20 A.M.

READ MORE COMMENTS ▼

---

[1] *technophobe:* someone who is afraid of, dislikes, or avoids technology
[2] *gossip:* informal talk about other people and their private lives
[3] *abbreviation:* a short form of a word or phrase

WRITING SKILL   Anecdotes

LEARN

Effective writers use specific examples to support an opinion or argument. One way to support an opinion in writing is to use anecdotes. An anecdote is a brief story about a person, event, or experience. Because anecdotes show an example that is true in the real world, they can help gain support from your readers. For example, in the writing models, each student described experiences with mobile devices in their classes.

To support your arguments with your own stories:

- think of an anecdote that shows your argument is strong or true.

- explain the main idea of your argument.

- introduce your anecdote. You can use a transition like *for example* or a clause such as *I remember when …* or *I experienced a similar situation.*

- describe the situation or circumstances surrounding your anecdote. Tell the important events of your story that support your opinion.

- use past tenses. Avoid unnecessary details. Keep your anecdote short.

- connect your anecdote to your argument and supply a reaction to the anecdote. How does the story support your ideas? How do you feel about the story?

APPLY

A. Match the main ideas to the anecdotes that support them.

___d___ 1. Some professors encourage students to use technology in class.

_____ 2. Technology can help students with their schoolwork.

_____ 3. Students should not come to class if they just want to use their smartphones.

_____ 4. Teachers should make students write in formal English.

    a. Some students write using the language of text messages.

    b. Annie improved her paper by recording her voice with her phone.

    c. Bill sees many students staring at their screens during class.

    d. Dr. Biedermeier was pleased when a student took a photo of the board with his cell phone.

B. Complete the chart using information from the models.

	Annie	Bill
Writer's opinion	*Cell phones improve the classroom.*	
Situation		
Events		
Reaction		

Analyze

A. Read Annie's post again. Answer the questions and discuss them with a partner.

1. What do the first two sentences tell the reader?

   _____

2. How many anecdotes are there in the second paragraph? _____

3. What is Annie's recommendation based on her anecdotes?

   _____

   _____

B. Read Bill's post again. Answer the questions and discuss them with a partner.

1. What is the purpose of the last sentence of the first paragraph?

   _____

   _____

2. How many different anecdotes are there in the second paragraph?

   _____

3. What is Bill's recommendation based on these anecdotes?

   _____

   _____

C. Discuss these questions in a small group.

1. Which student do you agree with? Why?

2. Which anecdotes do you find most useful? Why?

3. Do you have any anecdotes to share about the use of cell phones or other technology in class?

Vocabulary Activities | STEP I: Word Level

Noun	Verb	Adjective	Adverb
academy academic	_____	academic	academically
evolution	evolve	evolutionary	_____
maturity	mature	mature immature	_____
reluctance	_____	reluctant	reluctantly
rigidity	_____	rigid	rigidly

A. Circle the correct form of the target word to complete each sentence.

1. Schools should apply the anti-cell phone policy (*rigidity* / *rigid* / *rigidly*).

2. Teachers may be (*reluctance* / *reluctant* / *reluctantly*) to use new technologies.

3. High schools prepare students for college socially and (*academy* / *academic* / *academically*).

4. Opinions about the role of technology in schools have (*evolved* / *evolution* / *evolutionary*).

5. Good leaders need flexibility, not (*rigidity* / *rigid* / *rigidly*).

6. Teenagers often do not have the (*maturity* / *immaturity* / *mature*) to use technology responsibly.

B. Do the bold words have a positive or negative meaning in the context of these sentences? Circle *P* for positive or *N* for negative.

1. P / N Nancy is a true **academic**.

2. P / N He was asked to leave because of his **immature** behavior.

3. P / N He never **ceases** to try to improve.

4. P / N The company **overestimated** the sales of its new phone.

5. P / N The new director was famous for her **integrity**.

6. P / N All the students held **rigidly** to their opinions during the discussion.

Vocabulary Activities STEP II: Sentence Level

Survive can be an intransitive verb or a transitive verb.

1. An intransitive verb is not followed by a direct object. As an intransitive verb, *survive* means "to continue to live or exist."

   *Some animals can **survive** in very cold weather.*
   *Social media websites **survive** until something new comes along.*

2. A transitive verb is followed by a direct object.

               verb   diect object
   *Some businesses **survived** the financial crisis.*

As a transitive verb, *survive* means "to continue to live or exist despite something happening." It can also mean "to live longer than someone or something else."

   *My grandmother **survived** her husband by seven years.*

CORPUS

C. Some technologies *survive*, but others disappear. Do you think these technologies will *survive*? Circle *Y* (yes) or *N* (no), and discuss your ideas with a partner. Then write sentences with your reasons.

1. Y /Ⓝ   Television

    Why? _Television will not survive the growth of Internet videos._

2. Y / N   Smartphones

    Why? _____

3. Y / N   3-D printers

    Why? _____

4. Y / N   DVD players

    Why? _____

5. Y / N   Cars

    Why? _____

D. What do you know about these different generations? Write sentences and compare them with a partner.

1. your parents' generation

    In my parents' generation, many people got married at a young age.

2. your grandparents' generation

    _____

3. Generation X (people born in the 1970s and 1980s)

    _____

4. Generation Y (people born between 1980 and 2000)

    _____

The most common definition of *scenario* is "a description of how things might happen in the future."

*The most likely **scenario** is a restriction on the use of cell phones.*

Scenario is commonly used in the following phrases:

best-case scenario = the best possible thing that could happen

worst-case scenario = the worst possible thing that could happen

*The best-case **scenario** is that she gets an A on the test.*

CORPUS

E. Imagine that your school is considering a policy to restrict the use of cell phones.

1. Describe three possible scenarios. Discuss them all with a partner.

   One possible scenario is to allow cell phone use only between classes.

   _____

   _____

   _____

2. Which is the worst-case scenario? Why?

   _____

   _____

3. Which is the best-case scenario? Why?

   _____

   _____

4. If you disagree with this policy, what is a better policy for cell phones in your school?

   _____

   _____

F. Read each sentence. Write a question that the sentence answers. In your question, replace the underlined word with the correct form of *estimate*.

1. The flight's <u>expected</u> arrival time in Madrid is 5:30 p.m.

   What is the flight's estimated arrival time in Madrid?

2. In my <u>opinion</u>, Sanchez is the most skillful player on the team.

   _____

3. The mechanic <u>thinks</u> it will cost $600 to fix our car.

   _____

4. The <u>probable</u> shipping date for your order is September 29.

   _____

5. The professor <u>figures</u> it will take the students 30 minutes to read the assignment.

   _____

6. The landscaper was reluctant to give us <u>a quote</u> on the work.

   _____

Grammar | Modals

You can use **modals** such as *should, should not,* and *ought to* to give an opinion.

> Schools <u>*should*</u> teach computer skills.
> Students <u>*should not*</u> use cell phones during class.
> Teachers <u>*ought to*</u> ban cell phones from class.

You can use *must* or *must not* to make a very strong statement.

> You <u>*must*</u> switch off your cell phone.
> Students <u>*must not*</u> text during class.

Other modals can be used to show degrees of possibility.

> You <u>*can*</u> take a tablet computer anywhere.   **More possible**
>
> Electronic textbooks <u>*could*</u> become popular.
>
> Videos <u>*may*</u> become more common than text on the Internet.
>
> Cell phones <u>*might*</u> be useful in education.   **Less possible**

A. Match the sentences on the left with the meanings on the right. Meanings can be used more than once.

____ 1. People can access the Internet from computers, smartphones, and tablets.

____ 2. Families should not use cell phones during meals.

____ 3. Teenagers ought to pay for their own cell phones.

____ 4. Textbooks might become available on smartphones.

____ 5. Students in my English class must not use electronic dictionaries during tests.

____ 6. You should not check your email too often.

____ 7. We must send our assignments to the professor by email.

____ 8. Children must learn to have face-to-face conversations.

a. it is not allowed

b. it is possible

c. it is a good idea

d. it is a bad idea

e. it is necessary

B. What is your opinion about these ideas? Rewrite the sentences using *should, should not, ought to, must,* or *must not.* Discuss your answers with a partner.

1. Teach typing in schools.

   Schools should teach typing.

2. Use cell phones on airplanes.

   _____

3. Send text messages in a movie theater.

   _____

4. Use a cell phone to cheat on a test.

   _____

5. Use a computer to type your homework.

   _____

6. Charge your laptop battery every day.

   _____

7. Read textbooks on computers or tablets.

   _____

8. Answer emergency phone calls during class.

   _____

C. What will be some of the next big developments in technology? Discuss your ideas with a partner. Write sentences using *can, could, may,* or *might.*

   Cell phones could become thinner.

   You might read email on your watch.

   _____

   _____

   _____

   _____

   _____

   _____

   _____

   _____

   _____

WRITING SKILL | Writing a Thesis

LEARN

Discussion board posts and other types of opinion writing need a clear focus, or **thesis**. That is, they need a strong, clear opinion that writers support in different ways. Often, a sentence near the beginning (for example, at the end of the first paragraph) states the thesis. This focus then guides the organization of the writing. However, sometimes the writer's actual opinion is most clearly stated near the end.

To formulate a thesis, ask yourself these questions:

- What is the main topic?
- What is my opinion about that topic?
- Why do I think that?
- How can I support that opinion? Can I use an anecdote or offer examples or explanations?

APPLY

A. Does each sentence state a clear thesis? Discuss your answers with a partner.

1. Y / N   Many teenagers own cell phones.

2. Y / N   Some types of technology are really useful for students.

3. Y / N   Teachers should ban cell phones in class because students can use them to cheat.

4. Y / N   In the next ten years, students will cease using printed textbooks and will use electronic materials instead.

5. Y / N   The sales of desktop computers are declining.

B. What is the thesis, or opinion, of each writing model? Where is the author's opinion most clear?

Collaborative Writing

A. Choose one of the two writing models. Answer these questions.

1. What is the writer's opinion about cell phones in the classroom? What policy does the writer recommend?

2. Do you agree with the writer's opinion? Why, or why not?

3. What personal experiences can you use to support your opinion?

B. Work with a partner who has the same opinion as you. Write a reply to the discussion board post you chose in activity A. Use the outline to help you plan your reply before you write.

1. Background about the writers:

    _____

2. Thesis (opinion):

    _____

3. Anecdote:

    a. Situation: _____

    b. Events: _____

    _____

    _____

    c. Reaction: _____

4. Conclusions and recommendations:

    _____

    _____

C. Share your writing with another pair. Discuss these questions.

1. Does the reply have a clear opinion that responds to the original post? What is it?

2. Does the reply include at least one anecdote? Does it support the writers' opinion?

3. Does the reply include a conclusion and/or recommendation based on the anecdote?

Independent Writing

A. Choose one of the statements below. Complete the chart on the next page with ideas that agree and disagree with the statement. Then use the chart to help you form an opinion.

1. Every family should choose one night a week not to use the television, DVDs, Internet video, or video games.

2. Cell phones are harmful for young people.

For	Against

B. Once you've formed your opinion, think of an anecdote to support it. Answer these questions to help you describe your anecdote.

1. Where did it happen?

2. Who was there?

3. What happened?

4. What was your reaction to it?

5. Why does this experience support your opinion?

C. Answer these questions to help you develop your first paragraph, thesis, and final paragraph.

1. Why did you choose this topic?

2. What is your opinion? Write a sentence that explains your opinion and focuses your post.

3. What do your anecdotes show?

4. What do you recommend?

D. Write your discussion board post. Use your answers to the questions in activity C to help you organize your writing. Use modal verbs to give your opinions and recommendations. Use target vocabulary from page 99.

A. Read your discussion board post. Answer the questions below, and make revisions as needed.

1. Check (✓) the information you included in your discussion board post.

   ☐ your opinion as a clear thesis   ☐ a conclusion

   ☐ at least one anecdote   ☐ a recommendation

2. Look at the information you did not include. Would adding that information make your discussion board post more convincing?

Grammar for Editing | Subject-Verb Agreement

It is important to make sure that the subject and verb in a sentence agree. Third-person singular subjects (*he, she, it,* and all singular nouns) need an *–s* on the verb or a special form such as *is, has,* or *does.*

> Annie agree<u>s</u> with using cell phones in class.
>
> Technology <u>is</u> sometimes a distraction.
>
> <u>Does</u> the teacher allow computers in the classroom?

Modals are always written in the base form of the word.

> ✗ He <u>cans</u> email you the homework.
> He <u>can</u> email you the homework.

B. Check the language in your discussion board post. Revise and edit as needed.

Language Checklist
☐ I used target words in my discussion board post.
☐ I used modals to express obligation and possibility.
☐ My subjects and verbs agree.

C. Check the language in your discussion board post. Revise and edit as needed.

Self-Assessment Review: Go back to page 99 and reassess your knowledge of the target vocabulary. How has your understanding of the words changed? What words do you feel most comfortable using now?

UNIT 9

A Statement That Stands Out

In this unit, you will

> analyze personal statements and learn how they are used in university applications.
> use description and narration in your writing.
> increase your understanding of the target academic words for this unit.

WRITING SKILLS

> Analyzing a Conclusion
> Writing a Good Hook
> **GRAMMAR** Sentence Variety

Self-Assessment

Think about how well you know each target word, and check (✓) the appropriate column. I have...

TARGET WORDS	never seen this word before.	heard or seen the word but am not sure what it means.	heard or seen the word and understand what it means.	used the word confidently in *either* speaking or writing.
AWL				
🔑 authority				
commence				
🔑 credit				
🔑 fund				
🔑 investigate				
🔑 military				
neutral				
overlap				
🔑 prior				
🔑 seek				
🔑 survey				
unify				

🔑 Oxford 3000™ keywords

Building Knowledge

Read these questions. Discuss your answers in a small group.

1. Applications to colleges, universities, and even some jobs often require a personal statement from the applicant. Why do you think they ask for a personal statement?

2. What do you think people should write about in a personal statement?

3. If you were applying to a university, what would you tell about yourself? Why?

Writing Model

A personal statement is often required in a university application. The purpose of the statement is to describe who you are as a person and what makes you unique. Read a student's personal statement below.

Admissions Application

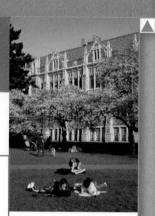

Personal Statement: *In your personal statement, explain why you are interested in journalism and why you wish to study at our university.*

In elementary school, I realized that I had two passions:[1] playing sports and writing. When I was younger, I was crazy about tennis. I played every day. I desperately wanted to become the next tennis superstar, and I truly believed I could. But by the time I got to junior high school, I accepted that tennis
5 *stardom was an unreachable dream. I practiced hard, but I just wasn't good enough. I am a very determined person, so I turned to my second love, writing. I loved reading the news, and I realized that my two interests **overlapped** in sports journalism. Therefore, I chose a more realistic dream. I planned to be a sportswriter for the high school newspaper the next year.*

10 *The summer before I started high school, however, my family had to move. Both of my parents are in the **military**, so moving was a regular disruption[2] in my life. At my new high school, I found out there was no student newspaper. I was*

---

[1] *passions:* very strong feelings of liking something
[2] *disruption:* a disturbance or interruption in a process

*shocked. Due to **funding** cuts, the school newspaper program was stopped. How could I **commence** my journey as a journalist without a newspaper? Some friends of mine and I **sought** the advice of our English teacher. We wrote a proposal for a new journalism class, and after much negotiation, the school administration approved it. Several months later, without any **prior** experience, we published our first newspaper issue. We were so proud!*

*I was the main writer for the sports page. I reported on our high school sports events and interviewed the coaches and key players. Sometimes I even traveled to games in other towns to cover the events. In addition to writing about sports, I also had the chance to report on regular school events and wrote quite a few opinion columns for the editorial page. I even interviewed school **authorities** for several articles. I **credit** my English teacher with encouraging me to try other kinds of news writing. In that way, I gained valuable skills.*

*My experience with the newspaper during the last three years has been difficult, fun, frustrating, and rewarding. I learned how to conduct a **survey** and publish the results in a colorful graph. I learned to put aside my own opinions and remain **neutral** when I **investigate** a story. I learned that a newspaper can **unify** a community because it encourages the discussion of important topics. Above all, my experience has inspired me to pursue a major in journalism.*

I chose to apply to your program because it offers a variety of courses in both journalism and mass communication.³ I still dream of being a professional sports writer. However, I would like to explore other areas such as advertising and broadcasting. It would be an honor to be accepted into your program.

---

³ *mass communication:* communication directed at a very large number of people, including via radio, TV, print media, or the Internet

LEARN

In writing, an effective conclusion ties together the main ideas of a piece of writing and ends on a strong note. In a personal statement, a conclusion is the writer's final chance to leave a positive impression on the reader.

Keep the following points in mind when you write a conclusion for a personal statement.

- Briefly restate or recap the main points of your statement.

- Relate your interests to what the university program has to offer. Be specific to show that you are familiar with the program or major.

- Mention skills or personal attributes that are related to your field of study.

- Include your career goals.

- Restate what makes you a strong applicant.

- Be sure that the points in your conclusion are supported by the body of your statement. Don't introduce new points.

APPLY

Reread the final paragraph in the student's personal statement. Analyze the conclusion on page 115 by answering the questions.

1. What are the main points that the writer makes in the personal statement? Are these points restated in the conclusion?

   _____

   _____

   _____

2. What evidence in the conclusion shows that the student is familiar with the university's program?

   _____

   _____

3. Does the student mention skills and personal attributes? Underline any examples in the model.

   _____

4. Does the student include career goals? Underline any examples in the model.

   _____

5. Does the student introduce any new points in the conclusion? Underline any examples in the model.

   _____

Analyze

A. Read each numbered item below. Decide whether to add it to the personal statement by answering these questions about each one:

- Should it be added to the personal statement? Why, or why not?
- If yes, where should it be inserted? Mark the position in the conclusion in the model on page 115.

1. I would bring to your program my passion for journalism and my determination to succeed.

2. During the past three years, my grade-point average was 3.8 and I received several academic awards.

3. I am especially impressed with your internship program. It reflects the value you place on learning by doing.

4. I am a very curious person and a strong investigative reporter, and I have good oral and written communication skills.

5. I don't feel ready to get a job yet, so I hope to continue my studies for a few more years.

B. Compare your answers to activity A with a partner.

C. Use the checklist below to evaluate each aspect of the model personal statement. Tell whether the author meets the criteria and add specific comments to support your response.

Criteria for a Strong Personal Statement	Y/N	Comments
1. The first paragraph is interesting and grabs my attention. It tells something unique about the writer.		
2. The statement focuses on one or two key ideas or experiences.		
3. The statement tells what the writer learned from experiences.		
4. The writer is familiar with what the university offers.		
5. The writer describes skills and personal attributes that are related to journalism.		
6. The writer describes career goals.		
7. There is a strong conclusion.		

D. In a small group, compare your evaluations of the writing model. Discuss the following questions.

1. What are the strongest aspects of the personal statement?

2. What are the weakest aspects?

3. Overall, is this a strong personal statement? Give reasons to support your answer.

   This personal statement is ... because ...

Vocabulary Activities | STEP I: Word Level

Word Form Chart		
Noun	**Verb**	**Adjective**
authority	_____	authoritative
investigation investigator	investigate	investigative
unification	unify	_____

A. Complete each sentence with the correct word form from the chart.

1. My professor is a leading _____*authority*_____ on coral reefs. She has published articles in many scientific journals.

2. In our history course, we are studying the 1990 _____ of East and West Germany.

3. After the accident, local residents asked for a thorough _____. The captain of the police department was the head _____.

4. Researchers found that teenagers with _____ parents have better grades than those with more permissive parents.

5. The new president hopes to _____ the country's many ethnic groups. Currently, these groups do not communicate well.

B. Match the words on the left and right to form common collocations.

____ 1. military	a. neutral
____ 2. politically	b. card
____ 3. prior	c. investigation
____ 4. credit	d. fund
____ 5. thorough	e. experience
____ 6. scholarship	f. vehicles

C. Complete the sentences with collocations from activity B.

1. The prime minister is sending _____*military vehicles*_____ to provide assistance to the region hit by the blizzard.

2. People use a _____ to buy things such as gas, food, and clothing.

3. The journalist conducted a very _____ into the town budget.

4. Local businesses donate money to the school's college _____.

5. It can be difficult for a person to get a job without _____.

6. That country doesn't get involved with wars or disputes with bordering countries. It's _____.

Vocabulary Activities STEP II: Sentence Level

Commence and *seek* are used in formal communication.

1. The verb *commence* means "to begin to happen or to begin something."

   She **commenced** military service in 2003.
   The ceremony will **commence** with a speech by the former president.

2. The verb *seek* has several meanings.

   a. to look for someone or something

      Due to the accident, drivers should **seek** alternate routes.

   b. to try to obtain or achieve something

      The city will **seek** funding for the new playground.
      I am **seeking** employment as a lawyer.

   c. to ask someone for something

      He left his house and **sought** help from a neighbor.

CORPUS

D. Rewrite the sentences using an appropriate form of *seek* or *commence*.

1. I'm looking for an internship with a law firm.

   I'm seeking an internship with a law firm.

2. I will start my graduate program next fall.

   _____

3. When will the ceremony begin?

   _____

4. Is anyone trying to find a full-time job in your office?

_____

5. The research began last October.

_____

6. I looked for a job that would give me experience in accounting.

_____

7. The candidate is trying to find support from young voters.

_____

Sometimes the noun and verb forms of a word are formed the same.

1. The noun *fund* means "a sum of money collected for a specific purpose."

   *The students are raising **funds** for a trip in June.*

   The verb *fund* means "to provide a project with money."

   *The government **funded** a new program for after-school sports.*

2. The noun *overlap* means "the parts of something that are shared with something else."

   *There is quite a bit of **overlap** between music and math.*

   The verb *overlap* means "to partly cover something else" or "to have parts that are shared with something else."

   *The topics in those courses **overlap**, so students should not take both classes.*

3. The noun *survey* means "a study of the opinions or behaviors of a group."

   *We conducted a **survey** to find out which sections were the most popular.*

   The verb *survey* means "to ask people questions for a study of something" or "to look at the whole of something."

   *The company **surveyed** over a thousand people last month.*

CORPUS

E. Answer the following questions, using the bold word in your response.

1. A public library is usually supported by **funds** from city, state, and federal governments. What other organizations do public funds support?

   Public funds can support public parks, schools, and law enforcement.

2. How do most college students **fund** their education?

   _____

   _____

3. Subjects and areas of study often **overlap**. For example, chemistry overlaps with math, especially when you do formulas and write lab reports. What are two other examples of subjects that **overlap**?

_____

_____

4. What are some examples of **overlap** between your favorite hobbies?

_____

_____

5. What kinds of **surveys** have you completed?

_____

_____

6. Imagine that you have to **survey** classmates about a new trend. What trend would you ask about? How or where would you **survey** people?

_____

_____

Grammar Sentence Variety

Sentence variety can make your writing more interesting. Here are some ways to increase sentence variety in your writing.

1. Use a variety of sentence types.

   a. Simple (one independent clause)

   My classmates and I published our first newspaper issue.

   b. Compound (two independent clauses)

   Our advisor assisted us, and we published our first issue a month later.

   c. Complex (one dependent clause and one independent clause)

   When I started high school, there was no student newspaper.

2. Use sentences of different lengths.

   I was shocked.
   In addition to writing about sports, I also had the chance to report on regular school events and wrote quite a few opinion columns for the editorial page.

3. Use prepositional phrases in a variety of locations. Note that prepositional phrases of time cannot always be placed in the middle of a sentence.

   During the last three years, my experience with the newspaper has been difficult.

   My experience with the newspaper _during the last three years_ has been difficult.

   My experience with the newspaper has been difficult _during the last three years_.

A. Read the following sentences from the writing model. Decide if each sentence is **simple** (*S*), **compound** (*CD*), or **complex** (*CX*).

_S_ 1. I was crazy about tennis.

___ 2. I am a very determined person, so I turned to my second love, writing.

___ 3. The summer before I started high school, however, my family had to move.

___ 4. Both of my parents are in the military, so moving was a regular disruption in my life.

___ 5. At my new high school, I found out there was no student newspaper.

___ 6. We wrote a proposal for a new journalism class, and after much negotiation, the school administration approved it.

___ 7. I learned to put aside my own opinions and remain neutral when I investigate a story.

___ 8. I still dream of being a professional sports writer, but I would also like to explore other areas such as advertising and broadcasting.

B. Rewrite each sentence two different ways by combining it with the prepositional phrase provided.

1. I always read the newspaper. / during breakfast

    I always read the newspaper during breakfast.

    During breakfast, I always read the newspaper.

2. The soccer team became very unified. / after the road trip

    _____

    _____

3. Sara's parents started a fund for her college education. / in 2008

    _____

    _____

4. Many of the graduates texted messages from their cell phones. / during the commencement ceremony

    _____

    _____

5. Due to my prior work experience, I found a job quickly. / after graduation

    _____

    _____

C. Check your answers to activity B by reading the sentences aloud with a partner.

WRITING SKILL Writing a Good Hook

LEARN

College admissions staff receive and read hundreds of personal statements, so you want yours to stand out. When writing a personal statement for a college application, grabbing the reader's attention at the beginning is important. You want the reader to be interested in your statement and read it to the end. One way to get your readers' attention is to start your statement with a *hook*. Imagine the hook on the end of a fishing rod: Its purpose is to catch fish, just as you want to catch the attention of the reader.

To write a good hook for a personal statement, think about your audience (an admissions officer) and the purpose of your writing (to reveal something personal about who you are). Which type of hook might work best for you?

- a story about yourself

- an interesting or surprising fact about yourself or an interest you have

- a definition or description

- a quotation or famous saying and how it relates to you

APPLY

Look at the hook in the writing model on page 114. What type of hook is it? Do you think it is a good hook? Discuss your opinions with a partner.

The writing model uses a ... for a hook. In my opinion, this is a ... hook because ...

Collaborative Writing

A. With a partner, read the following sample hooks. Analyze each one. What type of hook is it? Does it grab the reader's attention? Why, or why not? Write notes about each hook. Which hooks are the strongest?

1. The next best thing to playing sports is writing about them. As a child, my dream was to play tennis at the professional level. When I realized I wasn't going to be a star tennis player, I found a way to still be involved in sports: sports journalism.

_____

_____

2. Although the definition of a journalist is quite dry ("a person whose job is to collect and write news stories for newspapers, magazines, radio, or television"), I believe that a journalist is all about having a passion for people.

   _____

   _____

3. English writer Rebecca West once described journalism as "an ability to meet the challenge of filling the space." There are many times when I agree with West, but my ambition is to make news stories interesting, informative, and readable.

   _____

   _____

B. The paragraph below is the introduction to a student's personal statement. Read the paragraph. Then work with a partner to rewrite the paragraph by adding an interesting hook.

- Discuss the different types of hooks you could use.

- Discuss which type of hook is most effective.

- Work with your partner to rewrite the paragraph.

  I want to be a weather broadcaster on TV. I grew up in Florida, and I experienced many hurricanes as a child. I was fascinated with the weather prediction process. I loved watching the weather reporters. I started giving my own weather broadcasts to my family and friends. I made my reports informative and often funny. Everyone said I would be a great weather broadcaster. I started to believe them.

C. Share your new paragraphs with the class. Discuss how the hooks are similar and how they are different. Talk about which hooks are most effective and why.

Independent Writing

A. You are going to write a personal statement for an application to a university program. Think of what type of program you are applying to and why you have chosen that field of study. Brainstorm ideas. Fill in the idea map on the next page with words and phrases.

> **VOCABULARY TIP**
>
> Use positive adjectives to describe personal characteristics about yourself. Use a dictionary or a thesaurus to help you find some examples such as *ambitious, dedicated, independent,* and *resourceful.*

What makes me unique?
_____
_____

Key experiences?
_____
_____

PERSONAL STATEMENT

Career goals?
_____
_____

Why am I a strong applicant?
_____
_____

What motivates me?
_____
_____

B. Discuss your idea map with a partner. Decide on the best or strongest ideas to include in your personal statement. Mark those with a check (✓).

C. Complete the sentences in your own words.

1. I have been interested in _____ since _____.

2. _____ has always attracted me because _____.

3. I have chosen the _____ program at _____
   (university)

   because _____.

4. My experience in/at _____ led

   me to choose _____ as a career.

5. A degree in _____ will help me achieve my goals because

   _____.

D. Write two different hooks to start your statement. For each hook, write at least two sentences. Choose the best hook to include in your statement.

Hook 1: _____

_____

Hook 2: _____

_____

E. Write your personal statement. Use your notes from activities A–D.

REVISE AND EDIT

A. Read your personal statement. Answer the questions below, and make revisions as needed.

1. Check (✓) the information you included in your personal statement.

☐ a strong hook   ☐ a strong first paragraph

☐ one or two experiences   ☐ skills or personal attributes

☐ your career goals   ☐ strong conclusion

2. Look at the information you did not include. Would adding that information improve your personal statement?

Grammar for Editing   Subject-Verb Agreement

Sometimes the subject and the verb of a sentence are separated by a prepositional phrase. To check for agreement, circle every subject and underline the verb that goes with it.

studies

When my ⬚friend⬚ from the Philippines _study_ with me, we usually end up talking about food. (_friend_ is the subject, not _the Philippines_)

have

The newest ⬚members⬚ of the team _has_ to go to a special meeting with the coach. (_members_ is the subject, not _team_)

B. Check the language in your personal statement. Revise and edit as needed.

Language Checklist
☐ I used target words in my personal statement.
☐ I used adjectives to describe my personal characteristics.
☐ I used a variety of sentence types.
☐ I used correct subject-verb agreement.

C. Check your personal statement again. Repeat activities A and B.

Self-Assessment Review: Go back to page 113 and reassess your knowledge of the target vocabulary. How has your understanding of the words changed? What words do you feel most comfortable using now?

UNIT 10

Beating the Bug

In this unit, you will

> analyze blog posts and learn how they are used to deliver health information to the general public.

> use explanations in your writing.

> increase your understanding of the target academic words for this unit.

WRITING SKILLS

> Definitions

> Writing for Different Audiences

> **GRAMMAR** Personal and Demonstrative Pronouns

Self-Assessment

Think about how well you know each target word, and check (✓) the appropriate column. I have...

TARGET WORDS	never seen this word before.	heard or seen the word but am not sure what it means.	heard or seen the word and understand what it means.	used the word confidently in *either* speaking or writing.
AWL				
🔑 chemical				
converse				
🔑 exhibit				
ignorance				
🔑 mental				
mutual				
random				
🔑 reveal				
scope				
statistic				
supplement				
🔑 uniform				

🔑 Oxford 3000™ keywords

Building Knowledge

Read these questions. Discuss your answers in a small group.

1. If you don't feel well, where do you look for information about treatments?

2. Do you catch colds often? What happens when you have a cold?

3. Do you know what asthma is? If so, what do you know about it?
    Do you know anyone who has asthma?

Writing Model

An informational blog educates the general public online. Read about asthma on a college student health services website.

So, You Have Asthma?

You probably found this blog because your doctor told you that you have asthma. Asthma is a lung[1] disease. Asthmatics (people with asthma) **exhibit** several common symptoms,[2]
5 including coughing, wheezing, and difficulty breathing. Some people say that asthma is a **mental** condition—*it's all in your head*—but that's not true. Asthma is a real, physical illness that affects about 300 million people around
10 the world. Although there is no cure for asthma, you can live a completely normal, active life if you understand your condition and follow some simple advice.

WHAT'S IT LIKE TO HAVE ASTHMA?

"It's like breathing through a straw." That's how
15 many people with asthma describe their experience. Asthma causes inflammation of your airways. Airways are tubes that carry air in

and out of your lungs. When the sides of the airways become inflamed, they swell. This
20 means that there is less room for air to move through your airways, making it hard for you to take a deep breath. The inflammation also causes the wheezing[3] sound that all asthmatics know. As you can see from the
25 diagram on the next page, when your asthma is bad, you really are breathing through a straw.

---

[1] *lungs:* the organs in your chest used for breathing
[2] *symptom:* something that shows that you have an illness
[3] *wheeze:* to make noises when you breathe because of illness

Why do some people have asthma? We don't know for certain, but asthma is not completely **random**. If your parents have asthma, **statistics** show that you will have a much higher chance of being asthmatic. In addition, research has **revealed** common *triggers*, or things that cause an asthma attack, such as dust, pollen,[4] exercise, stress, and cold viruses. If you breathe in polluted air or certain **chemicals**, you can also develop asthma.

WHAT CAN YOU DO?

There is no **uniform** advice for all asthmatics, but doctors generally recommend three ways to control your asthma. First, it's important to know your triggers. That way, you won't get sick because you are **ignorant** of your own body! Every time your breathing gets worse, make a list of the places you have been and anything different you have done. Some common triggers are allergens (things that cause a reaction, such as dust, pollen, or pollution), irritants (things in the air that bother your lungs, such as smoke, strong smells, or cold weather), viruses (for example, the flu or the common cold), and exercise.

You can easily avoid some triggers. For example, some asthmatics can't wear perfume. Dust is hard to avoid, but you can buy a special cover for your pillow, remove carpets from your house, and vacuum regularly. **Conversely**, exercise is a trigger you should not avoid. Even though too much exercise might trigger your asthma, regular physical activity is important for all of us.

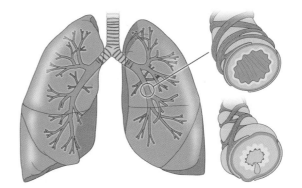

Airways become narrow when they are inflamed.

Doctors recommend asthmatics get at least 30 minutes of exercise every day. However, you should always exercise within your **scope** and stop if you have trouble breathing.

As a **supplement** to these lifestyle changes, many asthmatics take medications. This is the second way to control your asthma. It is very important to take your medications every day. They help prevent inflammation and make your breathing easier. Your doctor may change your medication if your asthma gets better or worse, so the final piece of advice is to monitor[5] your asthma. Write down any problems you have in a diary, and take it with you to your next doctor's appointment. Then you and your doctor can come to a **mutual** agreement about your treatment.

If you know your triggers, follow your doctor's advice, and watch your asthma—you can control your asthma!

---

[4] *pollen:* a fine, usually yellow powder that flowers produce
[5] *monitor:* to check, record, or watch something regularly for a period of time

LEARN

The writing model is a type of explanation. It tells about asthma and its symptoms, causes, and treatments. Explanations like this often include many definitions to explain words that the reader may not understand. Usually these words are specific to a topic. The author of the blog post defines words that are specific to medicine and to asthma, such as *trigger* and *inflammation*.

There are several ways to define words for your readers:

- State the definition: *Monitoring your asthma means checking it every day.*

- Give an example: *Monitor your asthma every day. Write down what you ate, where you went, what you did, and how your lungs reacted.*

- Put a definition in parentheses: *It's important to monitor (observe and check the state of) your asthma regularly.*

- Use *or*: *Doctors ask their patients to monitor, or check, their health daily.*

APPLY

A. Read the blog post again to find the meaning of the words below. Match each word to the correct definition. Discuss how the writer defined each word in the blog post.

_c_ 1. asthmatic

___ 2. inflammation

___ 3. trigger

___ 4. allergen

___ 5. virus

a. a condition in which part of the body becomes tender or swollen

b. a very small living thing that causes diseases

c. a person who suffers from asthma

d. the cause of a particular reaction

e. something that causes an allergic reaction

B. Complete the sentences using information from the writing model.

1. About 300 million people have asthma, *a lung disease* _____.

2. When asthmatics are sick, they often wheeze, or _____.

3. Many people with asthma keep a notebook with a list of all their symptoms

_____.

Analyze

A. How is the writing model organized? Complete the chart with words from the box.

| Inflammation | Statistics | Understand triggers | Genetics |
| Definition of asthma | Diary | Solutions | Medication |

Section	Purpose	Content
Introduction	Introduce asthma as a real, physical disease	1. _Definition of asthma_ 2. _Statistics_
What's It Like to Have Asthma?	Describe how asthma affects people and where it comes from	1. _____ 2. _____
What Can You Do?	Provide _____	1. _____ 2. _____ 3. Final encouragement 4. _____

B. Who is the audience for this blog post? Write **Y** (yes) or **N** (no) and give a reason. Discuss your answers with a partner.

1. _N_ Doctors

   Why? _The writer defines medical terms. Doctors already know the meaning of_

   these words.

2. ___ Young children

   Why? _____

3. ___ People who have just learned they have asthma

   Why? _____

4. ___ Parents of asthmatics

   Why? _____

5. ___ College students and young adults with asthma

   Why? _____

6. ___ Students in medical school

   Why? _____

C. Discuss these questions in a small group.

1. Did you find the blog post useful? Why, or why not?

2. What other information do you expect to find on a health services website like this?

3. Where else do you read explanations of complex ideas?

Vocabulary Activities STEP I: Word Level

A. Complete each sentence using a word from the box.

chemicals	exhibit	~~mutual~~	reveal
conversely	statistics	ignore	

1. I am very close to my brother, and the feeling is _____*mutual*_____.

2. I will now _____ this semester's top student: Mindy!

3. I love math, so I'm excited about learning _____.

4. I don't know why I did poorly on the test, but I could not _____ the problem.

5. You can come to class if you don't _____ any signs of the flu.

6. One symptom of the flu is a fever, or high temperature. _____, you don't usually get a fever with the common cold.

7. I don't like to eat artificially colored foods. I don't think the _____ are healthy.

The noun *scope* can be used in many different ways. It has the basic meaning of "a range of subjects or abilities." It also means "the opportunity or ability to do something." Notice the different prepositions.

> The **scope** <u>of</u> the new rule is very large.
> Healthy living is <u>within</u> everyone's **scope**.
> The challenge to increase food supply is international <u>in</u> **scope**.
> The problem of overeating is <u>outside/beyond the</u> **scope** of this article.
> There is **scope** <u>for</u> improvement.
> We have the **scope** <u>to</u> increase our knowledge of viruses.

CORPUS

B. Add *scope* + the correct prepositions to these sentences.

1. Your blog has _____*scope to*_____ grow by attracting new readers.

2. Your question is _____ of my job.

3. The _____ the problem is worrying.

4. Treatments for the virus are limited _____.

5. There is _____ more research into a cure for asthma.

C. Is the form of each underlined word correct (*C*) or incorrect (*I*)? Write the correct form for all incorrect words.

1. C /Ⓘ You need to be <u>mental</u> prepared before you go on a diet.

   mentally

2. C / I After the <u>reveal</u> of new information about asthma triggers, doctors changed their recommendations. _____

3. C / I It is a good idea to take a vitamin <u>supplement</u> every day.

   _____

4. C / I Some asthmatic children <u>ignorance</u> their first signs of difficulty breathing when they are playing sports. _____

5. C / I Research has <u>revealing</u> new ways to treat asthma better.

   _____

6. C / I A healthy body needs a healthy <u>mental</u>. _____

7. C / I Some people <u>ignorantly</u> do not accept that viruses cause colds.

   _____

8. C / I The doctor asked me for some <u>supplementary</u> information about my lifestyle. _____

Vocabulary Activities | STEP II: Sentence Level

As a noun, *uniform* means "a single type of clothes that a group of people wears, such as a school uniform or a police uniform."

> *Our basketball team is getting new **uniforms** next year.*

As an adjective, *uniform* means "the same in all ways and at all times." It is often used to describe rules (e.g., *standards, laws, quality*), physical qualities (e.g., *size, color, temperature, appearance*), and systems (e.g., *structure, guidelines, approach*).

> *The company's products have a **uniform** quality.*
> *Cut your vegetables into **uniform** sizes so they cook in the same amount of time.*
> *The university has **uniform** standards for all first-year writing classes.*

CORPUS

D. Read the announcement about a new program at your school on the next page. Then write your opinion about the ideas. Use the word *uniform* at least five times in your response.

Starting next semester, all students will have to meet the same standards of physical education before they graduate. All students must participate in the same three sports (swimming, cross-country running, and soccer). This single system will make sure that all students are physically healthy.

I agree / disagree with a uniform system of physical education because ...

_____

_____

_____

_____

E. **Discuss the questions with a partner. Then write a sentence to answer each one. Use the underlined word in your answer.**

1. Do you think it is useful to take vitamin <u>supplements</u>?

   I don't think vitamin supplements are useful because we can get all our

   vitamins from food.

2. What kind of <u>exhibitions</u> do you enjoy visiting?

   _____

   _____

3. Do you think students should choose their teachers, or should schools put students in classes <u>randomly</u>?

   _____

   _____

4. Did you wear a school <u>uniform</u> when you were a child? Do you think it is a good idea?

   _____

   _____

5. There are more children with asthma than adults (10 percent of children, 5 percent of adults in the U.S.), and the number of children with asthma is growing. What is one possible reason for these <u>statistics</u>?

   _____

   _____

6. Do you think diseases like asthma are <u>random</u>, or do they affect some people more than others?

   _____

   _____

Grammar | Personal and Demonstrative Pronouns

Pronouns are words that replace nouns. They can help writers avoid repetition.

> They
> It is very important to take your medications every day. ~~Medications~~ help prevent inflammation and make your breathing easier.

Do not use a pronoun if the meaning is not clear.

> ✗ The airways of asthmatics can become blocked because <u>they</u> are very sensitive.

In this sentence, *they* could mean *asthmatics* or *airways*, so it could be confusing.

Choose personal pronouns carefully. The writing model uses *you* many times because the blog writer wants to address the reader directly. However, in more academic writing, it is unusual to see *I, we*, and especially *you*.

> <u>You</u> should avoid <u>your</u> common triggers. (blog post)
>
> <u>Asthmatics</u> should avoid <u>their</u> common triggers. (academic paper)

Make sure you use object pronouns (*me, you, him, her, it, us, them*) after verbs and prepositions.

> me   him
> The doctor told ~~I~~ to bring my diary to ~~he~~.

Demonstrative pronouns (*this, that, these, those*) are very useful in writing. They can replace the last idea and help you create better cohesion. *This* is the most common demonstrative pronoun.

> Many asthmatics need to take medications. <u>This</u> is the second way to control your asthma.

A. Read the paragraph. Replace the underlined nouns with personal pronouns if the meaning is still clear.

The flu is a very common illness. (1) <u>The flu</u> *It* is caused by influenza viruses.

(2) <u>The viruses</u> infect the nose, throat, and lungs. When you have the flu,

you often have a fever, a runny nose, and a sore throat. (3) <u>The fever</u> can last

up to a week, and (4) <u>the fever</u> can make you feel very tired. Most experts

believe that flu viruses spread when people cough, so (5) <u>people</u> with the

flu should always cover their mouths. (6) <u>The flu</u> is not usually dangerous,

but (7) <u>the flu</u> can be life-threatening for children and the elderly. Asthmatics

should also be careful during flu season because (8) <u>asthmatics</u> can

experience difficulty breathing if they get sick.

B. Complete the sentences with the correct personal or demonstrative pronoun.

When I was a child, the doctor told (1) _____me_____ that I have asthma.

(2) _____ father also has asthma, and (3) _____ father

was asthmatic, too, so it runs in (4) _____ family. There are

often many asthmatics in the same family. (5) _____ is because

asthma is partly genetic. I had to see several doctors. (6) _____

recommended swimming as the best exercise, so I went to special swimming

classes for asthmatic children. We could all share (7) _____

experiences, and it helped (8) _____ , too.

C. Write a short paragraph about yourself and one other person in your family. Use personal and demonstrative pronouns in your paragraph. You can follow this example.

My brother and I are not very similar. He is tall, and his hair is dark. I'm short with light brown hair. He's interested in math and science, but I prefer reading and playing my guitar. However, we both like sports, and we ride our bikes everywhere. This means we spend a lot of time together.

_____

_____

_____

_____

WRITING SKILL | Writing for Different Audiences

LEARN

All writers need to think about their readers, or audience. The audience for the blog post in the writing model is young people with asthma. Therefore, the writer had to explain asthma in simple terms and define any medical vocabulary. The post also includes examples, a diagram, the pronoun *you*, and questions. An audience of doctors might not need this information, but they would want more supplementary details, such as the names of medications. Conversely, the writer of a personal blog might use *I* a lot and reveal anecdotes about his or her own experiences with asthma.

Ask yourself these questions about your audience:

- Who: What kind of people will be reading my post?

- What: What kind of background do they have? What do they already know? What do they not know? Do they likely agree with my opinions or not?

- Why: What is their purpose for reading my post? What is my purpose for writing it—what do I want them to know, think, or do?

APPLY

Imagine you are writing an article about asthma for a medical textbook. What would you add, delete, or change in the writing model, and why?

How does asthma cause breathing problems? Future doctors need to understand the physical and chemical processes more than patients.

Collaborative Writing

A. Choose a medical condition you know well to write about, such as a virus, an infection, diabetes, or migraines. With a partner, complete the idea map with as much information as possible. Add your own ideas.

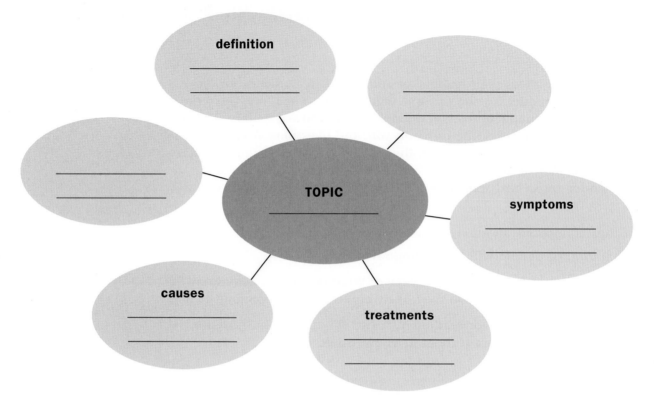

B. Work with your partner. Write an explanation of your topic for college students who are not studying medicine. You can use this structure:

1. Definition

2. Causes

3. Symptoms (with examples)

4. Treatments

5. Any other information

C. Share your explanation with the class. Discuss these questions.

1. Can a nonexpert audience easily understand your explanation?

2. What other information do you want to know?

3. Are there enough definitions?

Independent Writing

A. You are going to write a blog post for a student health website about the common cold. You will explain how to avoid catching a cold and treatments for it. First, brainstorm everything you know about the common cold, including treatments you have tried or heard about.

B. Read the list of facts below. What information will readers probably already know? What information will be interesting to your audience? Choose three or four facts to use in your post.

_____ 1. The cause of the cold is a virus.

_____ 2. People usually catch colds from other people with the cold virus.

_____ 3. You can buy medications for cold symptoms at any drugstore.

_____ 4. Being cold and wet does not usually cause colds.

_____ 5. Children have five to seven colds every year.

_____ 6. Common symptoms include coughing, sneezing, a runny nose, a sore throat, and feeling tired.

_____ 7. There is no cure for the common cold.

_____ 8. Some recommended treatments are sleeping, drinking lots of water, and eating spicy foods.

_____ 9. Anyone can catch a cold.

_____ 10. Cover your mouth when you sneeze to avoid spreading the cold virus.

C. Add an example to each sentence using _for example, for instance, such as,_ or _like._

1. Colds are dangerous for certain groups of people,

   _such as children and the elderly._____.

2. You can pick up a cold virus from surfaces

   _____.

3. There are some things you can do to treat your cold

   _____.

4. Some people have favorite foods when they have a cold

   _____.

5. There are some ways to prevent colds _____.

D. Write your blog post. Use your answers to activities A and B to plan your writing. Be sure to include definitions in your post to help the reader understand any unknown words. Use some target vocabulary from page 127.

> **VOCABULARY TIP**
>
> Use the following words and phrases to introduce examples: _for example, for instance, such as,_ and _like._
>
> _You can stop spreading the flu. For example, don't go to school or work if you are sick._
>
> _Some cold symptoms are similar to the flu. For instance, both illnesses cause a runny nose and headache._
>
> _There are simple ways to treat a cold, such as drinking plenty of water and getting lots of rest._
>
> _Some illnesses, like the common cold and the flu, come from viruses._

REVISE AND EDIT

A. Read your blog post. Answer the questions below, and make revisions to your blog post as needed.

1. Check (✓) the information you included in your blog post.

   ☐ definitions   ☐ examples

   ☐ causes   ☐ symptoms

   ☐ treatment   ☐ recommendations

2. Look at the information you did not include. Would adding that information make your blog post better?

Grammar for Editing   Sentence Structure

The structure of English sentences depends on the verb. Intransitive verbs have no object, but you often add a prepositional phrase. Transitive verbs have one direct object. Ditransitive verbs can take two objects (a direct object and an indirect object).

Intransitive verb: Accidents happen.

Intransitive verb with a prepositional phrase: Colds often happen _in the winter_.

Transitive verb: You should drink _water_.

Ditransitive verb: Doctors can give _you medications_.

B. Check the language in your blog post. Revise and edit as needed.

Language Checklist
☐ I used target words in my blog post.
☐ I used appropriate phrases to introduce my examples.
☐ I used personal and demonstrative pronouns correctly.
☐ I used intransitive, transitive, and ditransitive verbs correctly.

C. Check your post again. Repeat activities A and B.

Self-Assessment Review: Go back to page 127 and reassess your knowledge of the target vocabulary. How has your understanding of the words changed? What words do you feel most comfortable using now?

The Academic Word List

Words targeted in Level 2 are bold

Word	Sublist	Location
🔑 **abandon**	8	**L2, U6**
abstract	6	L3, U1
academy	5	**L2, U8**
🔑 access	4	L0, U6
accommodate	9	L3, U6
🔑 accompany	8	L4, U6
accumulate	8	L3, U10
🔑 accurate	6	L0, U4
🔑 achieve	2	L0, U1
🔑 acknowledge	6	L0, U7
🔑 acquire	2	L3, U4
🔑 adapt	7	L0, U3
🔑 adequate	4	L3, U3
adjacent	10	L4, U3
🔑 adjust	5	L4, U6
administrate	2	L4, U10
🔑 adult	7	L0, U8
advocate	7	L4, U4
🔑 affect	2	L1, U2
aggregate	6	L4, U5
🔑 aid	7	L3, U4
albeit	10	L4, U9
allocate	6	L3, U1
🔑 **alter**	5	**L2, U6**
🔑 alternative	3	L1, U7
ambiguous	8	L4, U7
amend	5	L4, U1
analogy	9	L4, U2
🔑 analyze	1	L1, U9
🔑 annual	4	L1, U6
🔑 **anticipate**	9	**L2, U5**
apparent	4	**L2, U5**
append	8	L4, U9
🔑 appreciate	8	L0, U8
🔑 approach	1	L1, U2
🔑 appropriate	2	L3, U4
🔑 **approximate**	4	**L2, U1**
arbitrary	8	L4, U7
🔑 area	1	L0, U6
🔑 **aspect**	2	**L2, U3**
assemble	10	L3, U6
assess	1	**L2, U4**
assign	6	L3, U9
🔑 assist	2	L0, U4
🔑 assume	1	L3, U4
🔑 assure	9	L3, U9
🔑 attach	6	L0, U7
attain	9	L3, U5
🔑 **attitude**	4	**L2, U4**
attribute	4	L3, U3
🔑 author	6	L0, U9
🔑 **authority**	1	**L2, U9**
automate	8	**L2, U5**
🔑 available	1	L0, U8
🔑 aware	5	L1, U3
🔑 behalf	9	L4, U1
🔑 **benefit**	1	**L2, U4**
bias	8	L4, U2
🔑 bond	6	L4, U9
🔑 **brief**	6	**L2, U4**
bulk	9	L3, U1
🔑 capable	6	L3, U7
🔑 capacity	5	L4, U2
🔑 **category**	2	**L2, U3**
🔑 **cease**	9	**L2, U8**
🔑 challenge	5	L1, U2
🔑 channel	7	L4, U3
🔑 chapter	2	L0, U9
🔑 chart	8	L0, U8
🔑 **chemical**	7	**L2, U10**
🔑 circumstance	3	L4, U3
cite	6	L4, U7
🔑 civil	4	L3, U10
clarify	8	L3, U8
🔑 classic	7	L3, U9
clause	5	L3, U3
🔑 code	4	L0, U7
coherent	9	L4, U6
coincide	9	L4, U6
🔑 collapse	10	L3, U6
🔑 colleague	10	L3, U1
commence	9	**L2, U9**
🔑 comment	3	L1, U5
🔑 commission	2	L4, U2
🔑 **commit**	4	**L2, U2**
commodity	8	L4, U10
🔑 communicate	4	L1, U3
🔑 community	2	L1, U4
compatible	9	**L2, U3**
compensate	3	L4, U8
compile	10	L3, U2
complement	8	L4, U9

🔑 Oxford 3000™ words

Word	Sublist	Location
complex	2	L3, U10
component	3	L3, U3
compound	5	L3, U10
comprehensive	7	L3, U3
comprise	7	L3, U1
compute	2	L1, U7
conceive	10	L4, U4
concentrate	4	L1, U2
concept	1	L3, U9
conclude	2	L0, U2
concurrent	9	L4, U3
conduct	2	L1, U5
confer	4	L4, U9
confine	9	L4, U4
confirm	7	L1, U10
conflict	5	L1, U10
conform	8	L3, U8
consent	3	L3, U7
consequent	2	L4, U7
considerable	3	L3, U9
consist	1	L1, U1
constant	3	L1, U7
constitute	1	L4, U1
constrain	3	L4, U5
construct	**2**	**L2, U1**
consult	**5**	**L2, U2**
consume	**2**	**L2, U6**
contact	5	L1, U3
contemporary	8	L4, U3
context	**1**	**L2, U4**
contract	1	L3, U4
contradict	**8**	**L2, U4**
contrary	7	L3, U8
contrast	4	L3, U5
contribute	3	L1, U4
controversy	**9**	**L2, U1**
convene	3	L4, U8
converse	**9**	**L2, U10**
convert	7	L4, U9
convince	10	L1, U9
cooperate	6	L3, U2
coordinate	**3**	**L2, U5**
core	3	L4, U1
corporate	3	L1, U7
correspond	3	L3, U2
couple	7	L0, U7
create	**1**	**L2, U7**
credit	**2**	**L2, U9**
criteria	3	L3, U3
crucial	8	L4, U4
culture	2	L0, U9

Word	Sublist	Location
currency	**8**	**L2, U7**
cycle	4	L3, U1
data	1	L0, U3
debate	4	L3, U5
decade	7	L1, U9
decline	5	L1, U6
deduce	3	L3, U3
define	1	L0, U6
definite	7	L4, U6
demonstrate	3	L1, U5
denote	8	L4, U10
deny	7	L1, U10
depress	10	L0, U10
derive	1	L4, U2
design	2	L0, U3
despite	4	L3, U10
detect	**8**	**L2, U1**
deviate	8	L4, U7
device	9	L0, U7
devote	**9**	**L2, U4**
differentiate	7	L3, U8
dimension	4	L4, U9
diminish	**9**	**L2, U6**
discrete	5	L4, U10
discriminate	6	L4, U1
displace	8	L3, U5
display	6	L0, U9
dispose	7	L4, U8
distinct	2	L4, U10
distort	9	L4, U7
distribute	1	L1, U6
diverse	6	L4, U3
document	3	L0, U10
domain	6	L4, U7
domestic	**4**	**L2, U6**
dominate	3	L4, U8
draft	5	L0, U10
drama	**8**	**L2, U7**
duration	**9**	**L2, U5**
dynamic	7	L3, U1
economy	**1**	**L2, U3**
edit	6	L1, U1
element	2	L3, U9
eliminate	7	L1, U7
emerge	4	L4, U10
emphasis	3	L1, U7
empirical	7	L4, U5
enable	**5**	**L2, U7**
encounter	10	L1, U5

🔑 Oxford 3000™ words

Word	Sublist	Location
energy	5	L0, U1
enforce	5	L4, U7
enhance	6	L3, U5
enormous	10	L0, U2
ensure	3	L4, U6
entity	5	L4, U9
environment	1	L1, U6
equate	2	L3, U2
equip	**7**	**L2, U3**
equivalent	5	L1, U10
erode	9	L4, U8
error	4	L0, U4
establish	**1**	**L2, U2**
estate	6	L3, U1
estimate	**1**	**L2, U8**
ethic	9	L3, U8
ethnic	4	L3, U10
evaluate	2	L1, U8
eventual	8	L3, U5
evident	**1**	**L2, U1**
evolve	**5**	**L2, U8**
exceed	6	L1, U8
exclude	**3**	**L2, U2**
exhibit	**8**	**L2, U10**
expand	5	L0, U2
expert	**6**	**L2, U2**
explicit	6	L4, U7
exploit	8	L4, U7
export	1	L3, U9
expose	5	L4, U8
external	**5**	**L2, U3**
extract	7	L3, U5
facilitate	5	L3, U6
factor	1	L3, U2
feature	2	L0, U5
federal	6	L4, U1
fee	6	L0, U5
file	7	L0, U10
final	2	L0, U3
finance	1	L3, U4
finite	7	L4, U9
flexible	6	L1, U10
fluctuate	8	L4, U6
focus	2	L0, U1
format	**9**	**L2, U1**
formula	1	L3, U8
forthcoming	10	L4, U9
found	9	L0, U10
foundation	7	L1, U9
framework	3	L4, U3

Word	Sublist	Location
function	1	L3, U3
fund	**3**	**L2, U9**
fundamental	5	L1, U8
furthermore	6	L3, U1
gender	6	L3, U2
generate	5	L1, U4
generation	**5**	**L2, U8**
globe	**7**	**L2, U1**
goal	4	L0, U1
grade	7	L0, U9
grant	4	L3, U2
guarantee	7	L1, U4
guideline	8	L1, U8
hence	4	L3, U1
hierarchy	7	L4, U10
highlight	8	L0, U7
hypothesis	4	L3, U7
identical	7	L3, U7
identify	1	L1, U5
ideology	7	L4, U3
ignorance	**6**	**L2, U10**
illustrate	3	L0, U6
image	5	L1, U7
immigrate	3	L4, U8
impact	**2**	**L2, U6**
implement	4	L4, U7
implicate	4	L3, U7
implicit	8	L4, U1
imply	3	L3, U5
impose	4	L3, U8
incentive	6	L4, U5
incidence	6	L3, U2
incline	10	L4, U6
income	1	L3, U2
incorporate	6	L4, U3
index	6	L4, U8
indicate	**1**	**L2, U3**
individual	1	L0, U4
induce	8	L4, U4
inevitable	8	L4, U1
infer	7	L4, U2
infrastructure	8	L4, U10
inherent	9	L4, U5
inhibit	6	L4, U5
initial	3	L0, U4
initiate	6	L3, U2
injure	2	L4, U6
innovate	7	L3, U3

Oxford 3000™ words

Word	Sublist	Location
input	6	**L2, U2**
insert	7	**L2, U7**
insight	9	L3, U7
inspect	8	L4, U7
🔑 instance	3	L3, U4
🔑 institute	2	L1, U8
instruct	6	L1, U10
integral	9	L4, U5
integrate	4	L4, U7
integrity	10	**L2, U8**
🔑 intelligence	6	L0, U8
🔑 intense	8	L3, U7
interact	3	**L2, U1**
intermediate	9	**L2, U7**
🔑 internal	4	L1, U2
interpret	1	L4, U2
🔑 interval	6	L3, U7
intervene	7	L3, U4
intrinsic	10	L4, U5
🔑 invest	2	L3, U9
🔑 **investigate**	4	**L2, U9**
invoke	10	L4, U9
🔑 involve	1	L3, U10
isolate	7	L3, U4
🔑 issue	1	L0, U6
🔑 item	2	L0, U5
🔑 job	4	L0, U3
journal	2	L1, U9
🔑 justify	3	L3, U2
🔑 label	4	L0, U5
🔑 **labor**	1	**L2, U4**
🔑 layer	3	L4, U10
🔑 lecture	6	L0, U8
🔑 legal	1	L1, U3
legislate	1	L4, U1
levy	10	L4, U4
🔑 liberal	5	L4, U3
🔑 license	5	L3, U6
likewise	10	L3, U10
🔑 link	3	L0, U5
🔑 locate	3	L1, U1
🔑 logic	5	L3, U1
🔑 maintain	2	L1, U4
🔑 major	1	L0, U2
manipulate	8	L4, U2
manual	9	L3, U3
margin	5	**L2, U4**
mature	9	**L2, U8**

Word	Sublist	Location
maximize	3	L1, U7
mechanism	4	L3, U3
🔑 media	7	L0, U9
mediate	9	L3, U4
🔑 medical	5	L1, U2
🔑 medium	9	L1, U10
🔑 **mental**	5	**L2, U10**
🔑 method	1	L1, U3
migrate	6	L4, U10
🔑 **military**	9	**L2, U9**
minimal	9	L1, U8
minimize	8	L3, U9
🔑 minimum	6	L1, U8
🔑 ministry	6	L4, U1
🔑 minor	3	L0, U8
mode	7	L3, U2
modify	5	L1, U10
🔑 monitor	5	L3, U7
motive	6	**L2, U4**
mutual	9	**L2, U10**
negate	3	L4, U8
🔑 **network**	5	**L2, U5**
neutral	6	**L2, U9**
🔑 nevertheless	6	L3, U10
nonetheless	10	L4, U6
norm	9	L4, U5
🔑 normal	2	L0, U3
🔑 notion	5	L4, U2
notwithstanding	10	L4, U2
🔑 nuclear	8	L3, U10
🔑 objective	5	L0, U4
🔑 obtain	2	L3, U1
🔑 obvious	4	L1, U5
🔑 occupy	4	L4, U6
🔑 **occur**	1	**L2, U1**
🔑 odd	10	L1, U1
offset	8	L3, U2
ongoing	10	**L2, U5**
🔑 option	4	L1, U9
orient	5	L4, U7
outcome	3	**L2, U4**
🔑 **output**	4	**L2, U3**
🔑 **overall**	4	**L2, U3**
overlap	9	**L2, U9**
🔑 overseas	6	L3, U10
🔑 panel	10	L4, U1
paradigm	7	L4, U9
paragraph	8	L1, U1

🔑 Oxford 3000™ words

Word	Sublist	Location
parallel	4	L4, U10
parameter	4	L3, U8
participate	2	L1, U1
partner	3	L0, U5
passive	9	L3, U8
perceive	2	L4, U6
percent	1	L1, U7
period	1	L3, U4
persist	10	L3, U7
perspective	**5**	**L2, U3**
phase	**4**	**L2, U1**
phenomenon	7	L4, U5
philosophy	3	L3, U9
physical	3	L0, U1
plus	8	L0, U6
policy	**1**	**L2, U8**
portion	**9**	**L2, U6**
pose	10	L4, U2
positive	2	L0, U1
potential	**2**	**L2, U5**
practitioner	8	L4, U4
precede	6	L3, U8
precise	5	L3, U9
predict	4	L0, U3
predominant	8	L4, U10
preliminary	**9**	**L2, U5**
presume	6	L4, U6
previous	2	L0, U5
primary	2	L1, U4
prime	5	L4, U6
principal	**4**	**L2, U7**
principle	1	L3, U8
prior	**4**	**L2, U9**
priority	**7**	**L2, U5**
proceed	**1**	**L2, U7**
process	1	L1, U5
professional	4	L1, U8
prohibit	7	L3, U5
project	4	L1, U1
promote	4	L4, U4
proportion	**3**	**L2, U6**
prospect	8	L4, U2
protocol	9	L4, U8
psychology	**5**	**L2, U6**
publication	7	L3, U7
publish	3	L0, U10
purchase	2	L0, U5
pursue	5	L4, U1
qualitative	9	L4, U5
quote	7	L1, U9

Word	Sublist	Location
radical	8	L4, U2
random	**8**	**L2, U10**
range	**2**	**L2, U3**
ratio	5	L3, U6
rational	6	L3, U8
react	3	L1, U5
recover	**6**	**L2, U5**
refine	9	L3, U1
regime	4	L3, U10
region	2	L3, U10
register	3	L3, U9
regulate	2	L3, U3
reinforce	8	L3, U6
reject	5	L1, U10
relax	9	L0, U4
release	7	L1, U6
relevant	2	L3, U2
reluctance	**10**	**L2, U8**
rely	**3**	**L2, U6**
remove	3	L0, U8
require	1	L0, U3
research	1	L0, U2
reside	2	L4, U4
resolve	**4**	**L2, U4**
resource	2	L0, U4
respond	1	L1, U4
restore	**8**	**L2, U5**
restrain	9	L3, U6
restrict	**2**	**L2, U6**
retain	4	L4, U8
reveal	**6**	**L2, U10**
revenue	5	L3, U9
reverse	7	L3, U4
revise	8	L1, U8
revolution	9	L4, U3
rigid	**9**	**L2, U8**
role	1	L0, U7
route	9	L3, U10
scenario	**9**	**L2, U8**
schedule	7	L1, U2
scheme	3	L4, U8
scope	**6**	**L2, U10**
section	1	L0, U2
sector	1	L4, U9
secure	2	L1, U4
seek	**2**	**L2, U9**
select	2	L1, U6
sequence	3	L1, U6
series	4	L0, U2
sex	3	L4, U5

Word	Sublist	Location		Word	Sublist	Location
shift	3	**L2, U7**		topic	7	L0, U7
significant	1	L3, U7		trace	6	L4, U10
similar	1	L1, U6		tradition	2	L0, U9
simulate	7	L3, U3		transfer	2	L1, U6
site	2	L1, U1		transform	6	L3, U1
so-called	10	**L2, U1**		**transit**	5	**L2, U2**
sole	7	L4, U4		transmit	7	L4, U10
somewhat	7	L3, U5		transport	6	L1, U8
source	1	L1, U6		trend	5	L1, U3
specific	1	L1, U3		trigger	9	L4, U4
specify	3	L1, U9				
sphere	9	L4, U2		ultimate	7	L3, U9
stable	5	L3, U6		undergo	10	L4, U4
statistic	4	**L2, U10**		underlie	6	L4, U5
status	4	L0, U9		undertake	4	L4, U3
straightforward	10	L3, U3		**uniform**	7	**L2, U10**
strategy	2	**L2, U2**		**unify**	9	**L2, U9**
stress	4	L0, U1		**unique**	7	**L2, U7**
structure	1	**L2, U7**		utilize	6	L3, U6
style	5	**L2, U2**				
submit	7	L1, U10		valid	3	L3, U8
subordinate	9	L4, U9		vary	1	L1, U2
subsequent	4	L3, U5		**vehicle**	7	**L2, U2**
subsidy	6	L4, U3		version	5	L1, U9
substitute	5	**L2, U6**		via	7	L4, U3
successor	7	L3, U8		violate	9	L3, U6
sufficient	3	L4, U1		virtual	8	L3, U5
sum	4	L3, U5		visible	7	L0, U2
summary	4	L1, U3		**vision**	9	**L2, U2**
supplement	9	**L2, U10**		**visual**	8	**L2, U7**
survey	2	**L2, U9**		volume	3	L1, U7
survive	7	**L2, U8**		voluntary	7	L3, U4
suspend	9	L4, U1				
sustain	5	L3, U6		welfare	5	L4, U4
symbol	5	L0, U10		whereas	5	L4, U5
				whereby	10	L4, U8
tape	6	L3, U5		widespread	7	L3, U4
target	5	**L2, U2**				
task	3	L0, U6				
team	9	L0, U1				
technical	3	L3, U6				
technique	3	L3, U6				
technology	3	**L2, U3**				
temporary	9	L0, U6				
tense	7	**L2, U1**				
terminate	7	L4, U8				
text	2	L0, U10				
theme	7	L1, U9				
theory	1	L3, U7				
thereby	7	L4, U6				
thesis	7	L3, U7				

Oxford 3000™ words